See What I'm Saying

What Children Tell Us Through Their Art

Dr. Myra Levick

Islewest
PUBLISHING

Contents

Acknowledgements vii

Introduction ix

What You Can Learn From This Book ix
Why Learn About Children's Art? ix
The Stages/Sequences of Development:
Ages 18 Months to 11 Years xi

1 What Children Reveal in Their Drawings 1

Creative Expression through Art 1
Some Common Normal Indicators 3
Some Common Warning Signals 7
The Influence of Cultural Changes 10
Normal Stages/Sequences of Artistic Development 10

2 How To Inspire Creativity 18

Encouraging Creativity in Children 19

3 Babble-Scribble Stage/Sequence: Around 18 Months to 2 ½ Years 25

The First 18 Months 25
18 Months to 2 ½ Years 27

4 Word-Shape Stage/Sequence: Around 2 ½ to 4 Years 31

Warning Signals at 3 35

5   Sentence-Picture Stage/Sequence: Around 4 to 7 Years   37

    4 Years... Warning Signals at 4...   37, 43
    5 Years... Warning Signals at 5...   47, 53
    6 Years... Warning Signals at 6...   54, 61

6   Fact-Fantasy Stage/Sequence: Around 7 to 11 Years   63

    7 Years... Warning Signals at 7   63, 71
    8 to 9 years... Warning Signals at 8 to 9   73, 78
    9 to 10 years... Warning Signals at 9 to 10   86, 95

7   The End of the Beginning   98

    Attending to Danger Signals   103

8   What You Can Learn From What I Do   110

    How The Art Therapist Works   113

Afterword: Foundations of Art Therapy   123

About the Author   127

Appendix: Sources of Professional Help   129

Bibliography   133

Index   137

Acknowledgements

The idea of writing this book originally was not mine, and from those who will benefit, the credit must go to my husband, Leonard. While I hesitated to confront this venture, he argued that over the years, many art therapists, including myself, have frequently spoken to parents' and teachers' groups, explaining what art therapy is, in simple language. It was his suggestion that I "translate" the text book I had published in 1983, *They Could Not Talk And So They Drew*, into words that could be easily understood by those who are primarily involved in caring for children. Accepting the challenge and completing the book, *Mommy, Daddy, Look What I'm Saying*, published in 1986, could not have been accomplished without his continual encouragement, patience, and love.

The late Israel Zwerling, M.D., then Chairman of the Department of Mental Health Sciences, Hahnemann University, also encouraged me to pursue this project and suggested that I include a discussion of normal children's behavior for each stage of development. This elaboration enhanced the original concept.

Others most helpful in bringing the original book to the public have been sincerely acknowledged in that publication.

Over the years, many parents, student therapists, child care givers who read the book communicated their interest in my revising the book. They suggested that it be published in a soft cover edition, making it more available to everyone involved in the care of children.

I want to particularly thank Sandy Hirstein, CEO and Publisher at Islewest Publishing, Carlisle Communications for hearing what was written and seeing what was said—and for making this revised edition possible. The Islewest Team is acknowledged elsewhere, but I want to thank Mary Jo Graham, managing editor, and Sharon Cruse, assistant editor, for their efforts on behalf of this work.

A special thank you to Dr. Herman Belmont, Dr. Paul J. Fink, Bobbi Kaufman, Dr. Maxine Junge, Dr. Hugh Rosen, and Dr. Sandra Graves—respected colleagues and good friends, who took the time to review the revised manuscript before publication.

Without the children, parents, and teachers who shared stories and pictures about and by their children, there could be no beginning of this book. To preserve confidentiality, I cannot mention their names, but they know who they are, and I thank them for their precious contributions.

My dear friends, Myrna and Harvey, Phyllis and Al, are not only my cheering section, but have helped keep me focused when I wanted to go out and play. Thank you.

Finally, I thank my mother, children and grandchildren, for their constant support and encouragement of my endeavors. They make it possible for me to work and to love.

Introduction

What You Can Learn From This Book

Anything created by someone—a drawing, a painting, a piece of sculpture—is a nonverbal message from the creator about his or her inner self and how he or she experiences the world. We have no difficulty accepting this obvious fact when we observe a painting by van Gogh or Picasso. However, we frequently ignore this observation when looking at the work of children. We assume that children's pictures are "innocent"—freely expressed and totally void of any "hidden meaning." However, as with all art, children's art expresses something about the child who created it, something which has meaning for the child. It is also important to remember that the meaning of an individual child's art work cannot be determined by simply searching the art. Qualified professionals, such as art therapists, will always seek information about the child beyond the work, and they will not indiscriminately draw conclusions solely from the child's art work.

This book is not designed to turn the reader into an art therapist who can expertly evaluate the drawings of children. It can, however, give those who care about children insight into children's drawings. By learning how to distinguish the various stages of artistic development that children normally experience, parents, teachers, anyone who is involved in the care of children, will have another way to actually see a child's intellectual and emotional growth.

Why Learn About Children's Art?

Art is important to children. It provides them with an outlet for creative expression that is uniquely their own. It helps them gain recognition and acceptance for their ideas and feelings. For the healthy child, art expression is a way to chart intellectual and emotional growth. For the learning-disabled child, who often feels inadequate, acceptance of the child's art-work may be the first step in helping the child toward self-acceptance. For the emotionally disturbed child, whose fantasies seem real, art provides a way to separate fantasy from fact.

Why should a child's art convey such significant clues? You need only to look around you for the answers. In our lifetimes, visual images have become powerful rivals for words. Images inform, educate, and entertain us.

The behaviors of children are given many names. The caregiver may call them good, bad, wild, sweet, bashful, shy, disobedient, or stubborn. No matter what terms we apply, a behavior can be a key to assessing a child's developmental well-being. Looking at a child's pictures is one method for identifying and evaluating these behaviors.

While the era of visual images was emerging, there were also great social changes. Within the past several decades the nuclear family has split like the atom for which it was originally named. Divorce has become the norm, not the sad exception. This has led to a proliferation of self-help groups that offer resources for not only the harried single parent, but also for that parent's confused offspring. In our society today, more and more mothers are working outside the home; those who are not are sometimes regarded almost with suspicion. While once the nearby extended family of grandparents, aunts and uncles provided additional emotional support, now these relatives are more likely to be found only at the other end of a long-distance phone call. Newspapers and television provide daily reports about battered and sexually abused children, many of whom will draw on paper what they would never be able to express in words.

Objects in a drawing represent the wishes and fears of the child who made the drawing, just as the events, actions and objects in a dream represent the wishes and fears of the dreamer. Uncovering the messages that children convey through art requires training and experience. The untrained eye is unaware of what is significant and what is not. Consider, for example, the house in Figure 1.

This drawing of a floating house (**Fig. 1**) was created by a 5 1/2-year-

old boy. To the untrained eye it would appear to be a typical child's drawing. The house has a door, windows, and a roof. To the trained eye of an art therapist, however, there are several things missing. There is no smoke coming out of the chimney—in fact, there is no chimney at all. There are no people in the picture and there are no other objects in the picture. Why, you might ask, is this significant? Maybe the house is heated electrically, or maybe its occupants have moved and the house is empty. Could this explain why it was drawn this way?— Most probably it does not.

With this picture, Kim is revealing many things about himself. He is telling us that he is not thinking and feeling the way most 5 year-olds do about themselves and the objects in their environment. We know this because he is not drawing the way most children his age draw. Kim's drawing alerts those who understand the artistic stages through which children move to stop and pay attention. He may be revealing his perception of his environment and a need that he is unable to express in words. In a later chapter, we will examine what that need might be, as we learn to identify these signs and recognize how children naturally express themselves at various ages.

The text and children's drawings found in this book will provide you with a frame of reference for understanding the artistic stages/sequences that children move through from about 18 months to 11 years of age. The focus of this material will help you understand what is normal creative expression for children at certain ages, while also alerting you to some departure from those norms that may indicate a problem. In regard to departures that indicate a problem requiring professional attention, the book will serve as a consumer's guide, telling you when and where to find professional assistance, and advising you how to judge the qualifications of those professionals.

The Stages/Sequences of Development: Ages 18 Months to 11 Years

It may seem surprising, but the drawings of normal children all over the world show developmental progress in similar ways, despite cultural or ethnic differences. Knowledge of this expected sequence is particularly useful in evaluating the stages of your own child's development, to determine whether it is normal and healthy or stressful emotionally or physically.

This book will cover the development of children between the ages of 18 months and 11 years, explaining how the pictures they draw serve as a mental "yardstick" by which to assess the state of their health and growth. We will discuss the progression of children's artistic development at different ages:

Through age 2, children begin to scribble and discover the look and feel of using crayons or pencils on paper.

Through age 3, children begin to outline forms within the scribbles, delighting in the discoveries of the circle and the square.

Through ages 4 and 5, children begin to draw images with a purpose in mind, and they will readily explain to you what those shapes and forms mean. The sun may become a face or part of a flower. The sun's rays may become arms, legs, ears, hair, and head decorations. Ears will become large, heads will be bigger than bodies, and hats will grace those large heads. Boats, cars, and houses will be formed from squares and circles. Picture ideas will come from fantasies, environments, and stories read or told to children—Peter will be there in the tree, figuring out how to catch that mean old wolf below.

Finally, the child reaches the first artistic stage of sex differentiation, where "Mommy" grows breasts right on the paper and "Daddy" does not. You will see how, at this stage, you can spot warning signs of emotional trouble, learning disabilities, and, in rare instances, brain damage.

Why stop at age 11? By the age of 11 years, children will have developed the basic skills they will use to cope with adult life. Unfortunately, by the preteen years many children also will have stopped drawing. In most schools, a child who has not demonstrated unusual artistic ability is not encouraged to pursue further art studies. Another deterrent is the fact that arts programs are often the first to be eliminated when school budgets are squeezed. In addition, preadolescent energy is more likely to be channeled into physical pursuits—sports, social dancing, and group activities. Although drawings can still be revealing at this age (and even through adulthood), they now must be considered in a completely different context, one that is beyond the scope of this book.

Chapter 1

What Children Reveal in Their Drawings

Would you like to know when a child you care about is happy? sad? excited? frustrated? angry? scared? Obviously any concerned parent, or anyone responsible for the care of children, wants to know these things. We are always looking for clues in children's behavior or asking for verbal explanations that can help us understand what they mean when what they do or say is not immediately clear to us. Even discovering clues and hearing verbal explanations may still not make it clear. But there is a whole set of clues that most parents and teachers overlook—the clues in children's drawings.

Creative Expression through Art

Normally, a child will take to paper and crayon like a duck to water. Children seem to have a need to draw and will communicate non-verbally through image making whenever given the opportunity. Most of us have forgotten our earliest years, but those who have been involved in caring for a small child know that each new experience and sensation confronting the child is unsettling, whether the immediate response is one of distress or pleasure. Putting that sensation or experience on paper, changing it, adding to it, crossing it out, and connecting it to known objects and events, all are ways of organizing and reorganizing what is new with what is already known. This is one way of mastering the process of growing up. It involves bringing order to chaos, which is also the work of the artist.

The artist creates order out of disorder. This disorder may be something the artist feels inside or something chaotic perceived in the environment. Whatever the source, the artistic image that emerges is one that is orderly and said to be "universally appealing." This term does not mean that everyone who looks at a given work of art will like it. It simply implies that the final product, the work of art, focuses the viewer's attention on the artist's subject, away from the artist's personal thoughts and feelings. The result is that the viewer will relate to the subject matter and not to the person of the artist.

Not all artists are totally successful in separating their persons from their art. We have all seen famous works of art and wondered what the artist was thinking. The concept of universal appeal is a simplification of the basic criteria for identifying a work of art. The criteria demands that creative expression must have "universal" rather than specifically "personal" appeal. The work of the artist is to transform, through the creative process, personal chaotic feelings and ideas into a work of art that has universal appeal. If we can understand this basic criterion for looking at works of art, we can begin to understand the significance of children's art. Through creative expression, all children at a very young age naturally begin to use drawings to organize the multitude of new experiences they encounter as they grow and to create a sense of balance within themselves.

I have led you from the artist to the child to remind you that the child in all of us was once a budding artist. The practicing artist is doing professionally what we all did so naturally as children whenever given the opportunity. A few more examples from the world around us might be helpful, but before sharing these with you, I want to dispel a myth. Some time in your life you may have heard someone say something like, "Artists are crazy." Whether you believed it or not, in order to appreciate the art in art therapy and the role of the creative process in mental health, this myth must be dispelled.

A truly disturbed—even though talented—artist is no more able to make order out of chaos and create an image that disguises personal torment than is a mentally disturbed person who is not artistically talented. Consider for example, an artist who many of you know from books and films. Vincent van Gogh has been described by some as "that crazy artist who cut off his ear." His biographers, however, tell us that when van Gogh experienced serious mental disturbances, he did not want to paint. Although he spent the last year of his life in a mental hospital, most of the paintings produced during that year were created when he was lucid and in touch with reality. Looking at van Gogh's works in chronological order over his last year of life, one can sadly see the deterioration of his artistic ability.

Unlike van Gogh, Pablo Picasso, another famous artist, did not suffer periods of personal torment that prevented him from creating. But we know his art work was influenced and affected by chaotic personal and world events. "Guernica," one of Picasso's most famous paintings, depicts his personal feelings about war. His incredible talent and mental stability turned these feelings about the chaotic nature of war, into an artistic, non-verbal statement that can be understood by anyone who sees this expressive, dramatic painting. Although "Guernica" conveys a sense of war's madness, it does so because it's creator was not mad, but clearly in touch with the reality of war.

Contrast Picasso with the very disturbed mental patient who often has a need to draw. One manifestation of mental illness is that the person feels helpless and longs to be a child again—to be coddled and protected. It is the childlike quality in these disturbed adults that elicits spontaneous drawings. These patients, too, are making order out of chaos, but it is a personal chaos and the images are often childlike, fragmented, and even bizarre. Their meaning is known only to their creator. Unlike the work of a professional artist, the image is personal. It does not hold universal appeal.

The budding artist within each of us as a child was not always allowed to continue to express itself freely and creatively. As healthy adults, we have learned to live without this avenue of expression. We found other ways to express ourselves. It is important, however, that we provide these creative outlets for our children. Children need to organize their feelings and thoughts as they develop, and a natural way to do this is through creative expression.

This chapter contains drawings that have been created by children whose artistic development is within the normal range of their chronological age. It also contains drawings that suggest the children who drew them fall outside their normal range of development. The accompanying explanations will help you to recognize imprints of creative expressions and the difference of these two sets of drawings. Later in this work, you will see examples of children's images which indicate that troubling issues may be surfacing. However, in every instance, you must look with caution. A drawing may tell you what a child is feeling, but a single drawing cannot tell you the whole story. Remember that, although a drawing can clearly tell *what* is happening, it will not necessarily tell *why* it is happening. Later, you will read examples of how the art psychotherapist works to discover the *why*. You will also learn what you can do as a parent, teacher, or a caregiver when troubling issues surface.

Some Common Normal Indicators

The following drawings illustrate some of the skills developed by normal children at different ages.

Gale, 9, shows us very clearly that she knows the difference between men and women (Mommy and Daddy) and the accurate size relationship between adults and children (**Fig. 2**).

At 4 years of age, a child should be connecting different shapes that begin to look like something recognizable. Hal has done just that (**Fig. 3**).

Figure 2

Figure 3

Rae, at 7, has no problem illustrating words in a way that tells us she knows what they mean. At 7 that should be a simple task (**Fig. 4**). Renee and Lewis, both 6 years old, and in the same school as Rae, are also capable of accomplishing this task, which includes drawing complete figures and recognizable objects, and illustrating feelings and actions, such as crying and jumping. (**Figs. 5 & 6**).

Letitia is 8 years old and in the second grade. Her choices of images to illustrate the words that her teacher assigned show how well she can stay within her own boundaries (**Fig. 7**).

Figure 4

Figure 5

Figure 6

Figure 7

The first thing children do when they learn to hold a pencil or crayon is scribble. Joey and Hal, aged 2 and 3 years, are developing their own styles of nonverbal communication. An example of a typical scribble for this developmental period is illustrated in **Fig. 8**).

Making fine line drawings and creating designs takes time. Nina, 9, has been able to do this when drawing her favorite butterfly (**Fig. 9**).

Handling paints takes time too. Hal was just 3 when he started to use them. It is evident from his first efforts that he has not been very adept, but at 3 he is not expected to be (**Fig. 10**).

Figure 9

A demon that has eyes.

Figure 8

Figure 10

Dayna, age 4, is beginning to try to make figures by connecting the lines and circles she mastered when she was doing a lot of scribbling. You can still see some of the scribbles in this picture (**Fig. 11**).

Becca, at 5 1/2, is trying to tell us a story about a house, a car, the sun, and the sky (**Fig. 12**). Becca's house is firmly on the ground, telling us she is drawing normally for her age.

Some Common Warning Signals

At this point we will present some common warning signals found in children's drawings. Later, the implications of these signals will be discussed in detail.

There are several reasons for concern in this picture by 7-year-old Rafe (**Fig. 13**). First, the drawing generally looks like one that normally would be produced by a younger child. Second, Rafe's lines are shaky. He cannot seem to stay within his own boundaries.

Another child, Arthur, at age 6, should be able to draw recognizable objects. He is able to say what he wanted to draw, but his graphic productions show that he is not able to draw a single object that resembles his verbal descriptions (**Fig. 14**).

Figure 12

Figure 11

Figure 13

Figure 14

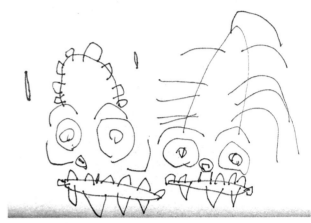

Bobby, at age 3, drew at every opportunity. Every image of a face has a huge gaping mouth, and it does not matter whether the face was supposed to be a monster, Mommy or Daddy. A repeated consistent form produced over and over as Bobby does, is a warning signal. An example of this repeated form is seen in **Fig. 15**.

Figure 15

Inconsistencies within the same picture demand our attention and concern. Lori, 10, draws one figure that is typical of a 10-year-old, yet in the same drawing the second figure and the house are so different that they could have been drawn by another child (**Fig. 16**).

Figure 16

We have already discussed Kim's floating house (**Fig. 1**), and identified the elements that make it a warning signal. Kitty, 9, draws circles around floating figures (**Fig. 17**). The figures of the family members are drawn well for a 9-year-old, but isolating each member in a bubble should be viewed as a warning signal.

Figure 17

Figure 18

Figure 19

Elaine, at the same age as Kitty, draws the figures of her family members with complete heads and very strange and incomplete bodies. The warning signal flashes when a 9-year-old omits body parts (**Fig. 18**).

Slanted images at any age need to be investigated. Rafe, 7, has drawn a house that appears to be falling (**Fig. 19**). Stu, 9 years old, draws himself and his "Mom" (**Fig. 20**). Like Rafe's house, the figures also look as though they are falling over.

The story a picture tells may be a recognizable symbol of danger. Owen, 9, has drawn a killer whale dripping blood (**Fig. 21**). It is possible that he has just seen a TV program or movie involving a killer whale. But, he may have a serious problem.

Once again we must emphasize that what is in a picture does not necessarily tell us why. All of these pictures flashed signals that said "check out this child." The most skilled and experienced art psychotherapist would not make a judgment based on only a drawing. Much more would need to be learned about each child before the therapist could conclude that there was, or was not, a specific problem. But those working with a young child have a context within which to try to understand the clues seen in drawings. Although these clues are not answers, they can lead us to ask the proper questions. In the chapters discussing the different age groups in depth, we will return to these drawings, reporting more information about each child and, when appropriate, what interventions were implemented.

Figure 20

Figure 21

The Influence of Cultural Changes

Children in all parts of the world begin to draw in the same way; later we will describe this process in detail. For now it is important to know that there are normal ranges of artistic development, allowing us to evaluate whether a drawing is appropriate for a particular child's age level. In making this evaluation we must also be aware of cultural influences and the ages at which children begin to include these influences in their drawings. Finally, we need to remember that our society is changing constantly, resulting in changes in normal developmental images. Television, for example, has impacted on our understanding of normal developmental images.

When I first began practicing art therapy in the 1960s, while television was still enjoying its innocence, I learned that most children draw stick figures at about age 7. This was expected behavior, because children this age usually are not interested in differentiating between the sexes. Between 7 and 10 years, most children are interested primarily in school and playing with their peers. They learn that the stick figure is an accepted representation of the human form.

In the 1970s, changes in the stick figures became noticeable. Children between ages 7 and 9 were beginning to draw sexual characteristics on their figures, differentiating between male and female. I began to question whether these children were precocious or being exposed to adult sexual behavior. To explore this phenomenon, I contacted colleagues in other parts of the country and discovered that they were observing the same changes. We finally concluded that it was becoming natural for children to draw sexual characteristics at an earlier age than in the past because children were seeing an emphasis on female/male characteristics/differences on television—not only in the regular programming, but also in the commercials. As society continues to change, it will be more and more common to see these changes reflected in children's drawings.

Normal Stages/Sequences of Artistic Development

The rest of this chapter will summarize what can be expected from a child at each major stage of artistic development, with examples of typical drawings for each stage/sequence. Then Chapters 3 through 6 will cover these periods of development in greater detail. The relationship among emotional development, intellectual development, and creative expression charted by the growing child through artworks will become clearer for you as we continue to explore the wonderful world of children's pictures. Before learning how the normal stages of artistic development are typically described, you should be aware that many art psychotherapists and psychologists do not totally accept the concept of "stages" of development.

A stage, in psychological terms, generally implies that a period of development has a definite beginning and ending. When discussing children, however, experience teaches us that not all children develop at the same pace. This does not mean that the slower child is less bright or less skilled, but only that for some reason this child is traveling along the path of development differently than most children. We also know that certain skills must be mastered before a child can learn a new task. This is particularly true in developing skills in drawing, and I believe that it is also true in intellectual development. As children are learning new skills they are still practicing and perfecting skills learned previously. Therefore, rather than use the term "stage," I will use the term "stage/sequence." Ages given for each period will be meant only as general guidelines. A developmentally normal child may perform the certain skills a little earlier or later with no cause for concern.

Babble-Scribble Stage/Sequence: About 18 months to 2 1/2 years

Between 18 months and 2 1/2 years, children are developing the ability to grasp objects and move them around. Given paper and crayon, they will delight in creating lines of different lengths and see-

Figure 22

ing them emerge in different directions. There is no apparent rhyme or reason to these early scribblings, just the sheer joy in the movement and the image. As the child gains greater body control, the lines begin to take form. A child may name an object if prompted by an adult.

Doug was 2 years and 1 month old when he drew **Fig. 22,** and Hal a little past 2 when he did **Fig. 23.**

Figure 23

Word-Shape Stage/Sequence: About 2 1/2 to 4 years

At the Word-Shape Stage/Sequence, the child begins to outline forms within the scribbles. Just as words are expressed randomly at first, shapes appear randomly. Very gradually these shapes become familiar circles and squares. Children begin to draw with a plan in mind. Depending on the amount and variety of stimulation in the environment and the availability of materials, they will produce drawings that are more or less complex. They will experiment with combining different shapes but often will not know what they are drawing until the work is finished. If asked, they will tell a story about their drawing.

Hal, at 3 years of age, has been experimenting with paints. He also had discovered he could combine circles with lines. When asked, he said one of his creations was a "crawling bug" and another "flowers" (**Figs. 24 and 25**). Feeling a little more adventurous, Molly is using magic markers, crayons, and paint to create this picture of structured images (**Fig. 26**).

Figure 24

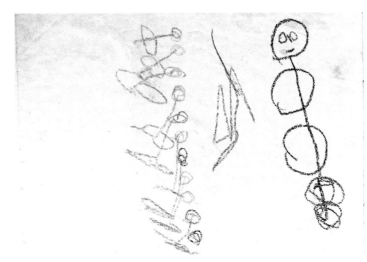

Figure 25

Figure 26

Figure 27

Figure 28

Figure 29

Indira and Gamal, both 3-year-old children from India, experimented with paints in the same way as their American counterparts do (Fig. 27). Although they did not say what they had created, their paintings are very similar to Hal's productions.

Sentence-Picture Stage/Sequence: About 4 to 7 years

At ages 4 to 7, children learn to complete simple sentences and draw pictures that tell a simple story. During this time, they become more aware of and are more influenced by their culture and environment.

Age 4: Scott has mastered the ability to draw a circle and to connect circles and lines to create a face-like image (Fig. 28). Bobby, also 4, has been able to combine lines, scribbles, and circles to create different people-like images (Fig. 29).

Figure 30

Age 5: Scott's mastery of all the things he has learned before helped him to create more complete figures with all the body parts and even (scribble) hair. Scott's growing ability is illustrated in **Fig. 30**.

Age 6: Scott and Lilly have moved into what is known as the pictorial stage. Scott combines his knowledge of shapes and lines to draw a picture of a house, a tree, and a person (**Fig. 31**). Lilly is more interested in using her knowledge and skill at this time to draw a sun, a huge flower, and a girl with a big bow on her head (**Fig. 32**). We expect to see all the body parts around this time, but it is not unusual for them to be distorted. One leg bigger than the other is not surprising and may even be expected; we will explain why in Chapter 6.

Figure 31

Figure 32

Figure 33

Figure 34

Fact-Fantasy Stage/Sequence: About 7 to 11 years

By about age 7, children have acquired many facts about the important people in their environment, and have developed fantasies about their world. They should be able to draw realistically and to improve on this skill continually. Their drawings should reflect their feelings, thoughts, and fantasies prompted by their surroundings. Drawings provide an appropriate and natural way for children in this age group to deal with the newness of school and peer interactions.

Age 7: Brad's illustrations all show his rich combinations of reality and fantasy, especially his picture of the teacher behind the desk shouting "NO" **(Fig. 33)**.

Age 7 1/2: Scott does not like snowmen, and one way to deal with this is to make the snowman a robot that he can control. He draws a white robot marching down snow covered hills **(Fig. 34)**.

Figure 35

Age 8: Nina and John show the ability to handle pencil and crayon, to draw realistically, and to use imagination to create original responses to a second-grade assignment. Their choices of examples to illustrate the words reflect familiar things in their environment (**Figs. 35 and 36**).

Figure 36

Figure 37

Figure 38

Figure 39

Age 9-10: Randy, age 9, can represent his ideas so well by now that he enjoys drawing fanciful images to illustrate those ideas (**Fig. 37**). Sue, 10, is able to draw people of all different ages realistically enough for us to recognize everyone in her "nice" family portrait and to make a clear distinction between males and females (**Fig. 38**). Herb, 9 1/2, has been drawing war scenes, which are very typical for boys this age (**Fig. 39**).

These examples illustrate the most common kinds of images we see sequentially in drawings of children who are growing normally. The children who produced these drawings are all physically well, functioning in the appropriate school grade for their age. This small sampling represents children from different socioeconomic groups, different religions, different races and different parts of the world.

This brief outline of the important stages/sequences of growth includes only normal developmental sequences. Each child is unique and grows at his or her own pace. Manifestations of abnormal development at any stage/sequence cannot be defined easily without considering the child's physical history from birth, in addition to the home and school environment at the time those warning signals appear.

There is a definite relationship between intelligence and artistic expression. A child cannot draw an object before being able to identify it intellectually. Normal intellectual development provides the child with the skills necessary to draw more recognizable objects. As the child learns more, drawings of objects become more detailed. Drawings are one way to measure intellectual development.

The next chapters, which discuss each age group, will demonstrate how a knowledge of normal stages/sequences of development helps us to determine whether a child is facing developmental stresses normal for that age or whether the danger signals we see suggest far more serious problems.

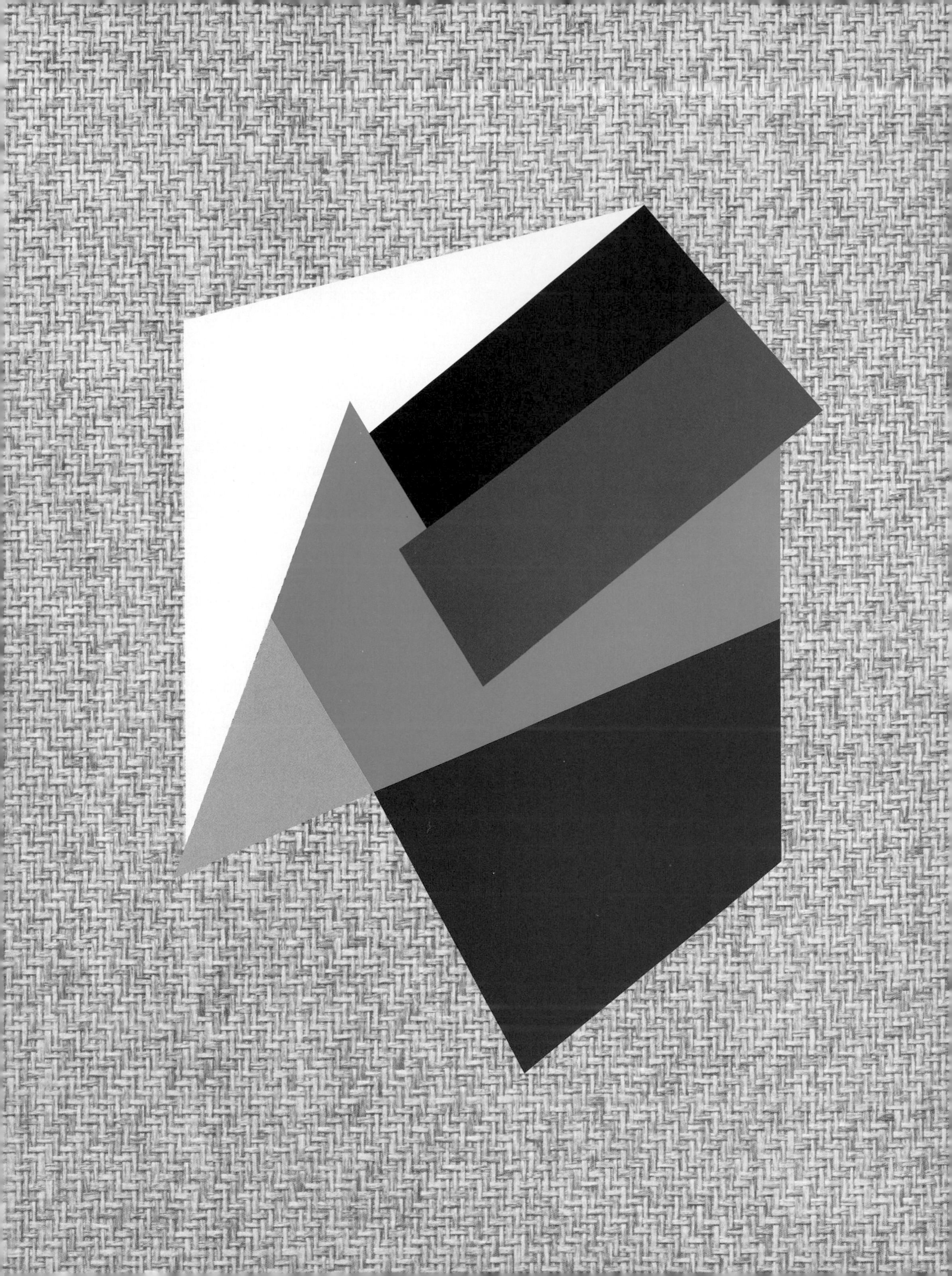

Chapter 2

How to Inspire Creative Expression

Acting creatively is essential to successful everyday living. Children are naturally creative. This creativity must be encouraged if they are to learn to express themselves freely and develop skills required for intellectual and emotional growth. This chapter offers recommendations to help you create an atmosphere in which this free expression can occur. We will suggest what kinds of media should be available at various ages and what you can do to stimulate a child's natural creative expression. We will also discuss what not to do—things parents and teachers do and say that can inhibit this expression and that make children self-conscious about their artistic endeavors.

Encouraging Creativity in Children

The word sublimation is familiar to most of us. However, the meaning of this word is often disputed by mental health professionals and is frequently misused. Most psychologists accept a definition of sublimation as the ability to obtain pleasure in a socially acceptable way. This explanation of sublimation relates closely to the creative process. Frequently, students of psychology are given this example of sublimation: "The artist is considered a well-sublimated person. The artist has learned to repress the infantile desire to smear, replacing it with the pleasure obtained through painting or sculpturing."

The artists in our art therapy classes bristle at the notion that artists are adults who have found a socially acceptable way to smear. I try to help them over this hurdle by sharing a story my mother enjoyed telling—one that I could not appreciate until I began to learn more about psychology. At about age 2, I discovered a way to peel off sections of wallpaper and dig out the plaster underneath. I would then entertain myself by playing with the plaster—rolling it, molding it, and even tasting it. Obviously, such behaviors could not be allowed for too long. It must have been around this time that my mother began to provide me with art materials. From then on, I drew constantly, and whatever I produced was accepted, praised, and saved. I had started the process of sublimation.

Over the years we have learned a great deal about the process and significance of sublimation. Early psychiatrists and psychologists thought that sublimation was a way of coping with anxiety. In more recent times, however, it has been considered a normal function of the healthy individual—a capacity present in all of us from birth. In other words, sublimation is not only an integral part of the artist's creative process. As for example, an especially curious child, who destroys every toy in an effort to discover how it works, may eventually sublimate this aggressive urge by pursuing a career as a research scientist—discovering why or how things work as they do.

There are many other examples of sublimation. What we need to understand for the purpose of this book is why, if we are all born with this capacity, some people seem to have it while others do not. Far from being an unnatural way of satisfying base urges, sublimating is the normal way most people achieve balance between their own desires and the demands of living in society. This ability to find alternate acceptable ways to gratify our most primitive wishes needs to be nurtured. This nourishment should begin with the earliest caregivers: mothers, fathers or anyone else involved in creating the environment in which the child is growing.

There are specific developmental tasks that must be achieved before a child can take crayon in hand and begin to learn the fun of making images on paper. These will be covered in detail in the next chapter. For now we will discuss the kind of environment that is necessary in order for children to begin creating.

First, any art activity should take place in a safe area in which the child can explore art materials. The very young child should be able to move freely. Attention spans are short in these early years, and we must remember that the child may lose interest in something in a very brief period of time. When the child is a little older, the "art area" should allow for spilling or cutting or pasting. This area need not be one devoted exclusively to the child—it can be the kitchen table, the basement floor, or the outside porch. A good place is any that provides freedom to use the art materials in an unrestricted and individual way.

Regardless of the child's age, production should be encouraged and the art works valued. Also the child's wishes about what happens to those art productions should be respected. This is not to say that the works must be displayed in areas that are not acceptable to the rest of the family, but there should be a place to show the artwork and a place to store them. Showing respect for the child's work is a way to help children to begin to respect the property rights of others. For the same reason, very young siblings should be allowed to have their own sets of materials and their own space.

I know too well how difficult it is for the teacher, whether in a preschool, elementary school or junior high school, to provide individual freedom of artistic expression in a classroom of twenty or more children. Whatever the physical restrictions, however, teachers are responsible for helping students achieve many goals. Teachers will demonstrate how to use various media, and they help students learn how to draw objects in the environment so that the images produced are aesthetically pleasing. All of these goals are necessary steps in the learning process. Every new task a child masters provides skills that can be applied to a variety of other learning tasks. But children should not be expected to complete all assignments in the same "cookie cutter" way. I remember one first grade student who decided to make her tree trunk purple and the leaves brown. Although the student teacher had no special training in art or art therapy, she did know that individual expression was to be encouraged and, fortunately, responded to this image with the same enthusiasm she showed when looking at more realistically colored trees.

Once, at a social gathering, I met a woman who told me how pleased she was with her son's art teacher in junior high school. When she mentioned the teacher by name, I recognized it immediately. He was an artist who had consulted me for psychotherapy while completing his education for certification as an art teacher. The woman described how he made the weekly art class an exciting event for the children by providing a variety of materials such as pieces of cloth, wood, and shells, in addition to paints and clay. The children were invited to create whatever they wanted, either individually or working with other classmates. Special help was provided to students who were unfamiliar with certain supplies. Each piece of art produced by his students was accepted by this teacher as a unique and special creation. When I called to report the nice things I had been told about his teaching methods, he said that his experience in art therapy had made him realize how valuable it is to encourage the creative process rather than emphasize the final art product.

Not all art teachers can be or should be art therapists, but all teachers should provide a climate for individual expression. Speaking with teachers at conferences over the years, I know that more and more teachers are becoming aware of this need. They are working very hard to change rigid approaches to teaching art, such as requiring everyone in a class to produce the same image in the same way. Art teachers and art therapists have established task forces in which representatives from each group share ideas on how to help children grow through art expression. Teachers and art therapists are also defining their individual roles and responsibilities in this process.

While a favorable environment is the first element necessary for free expression, second is providing the tools to create that expression. Children can learn to express themselves at a very early age with any materials available. Infants and toddlers have an instinctive desire to play with food, mud, and sand simply because they enjoy the feel of these elements and derive pleasure from the newly gained control over body movement. It is obvious that around age of 18 months to 2 years, the child recognizes simple commands, such as the meaning of "no." When the toddler can understand such simple directions, grasp small objects, and control arm movement, it is time to provide crayons and paper.

Big, fat crayons are probably best in the beginning, as these can be managed easily by small hands. Any inexpensive paper is fine. Large pads of newsprint are good, but you can use almost any kind of paper available around the house, so long as one side of it is blank. The only caution is to be sure that any coloring on the paper is nontoxic. Toddlers sometimes enjoy crumpling and tasting the paper as much as coloring on it. They may also want to taste the crayons, just as they may have tasted sand or mud. When children are this young, you need to supervise and show the child how these new objects should be handled. Sit down on the floor and scribble with the child—yes, scribble. Watching and imitating you is the beginning of learning how to be a grown-up person.

If a child has no physical impairments, dexterity will naturally increase. When a child reaches age 4 or 5, you may want to teach how to cut with blunt scissors. Construction paper is wonderful for this purpose. Throughout the child's artistic development, you must be patient and observant. Children will let you know when they are ready to try new and more complicated art supplies.

Paint can be introduced as early as 3 years of age. Large jars of tempera paint and wide brushes can be purchased at a hobby or toy shop. Be sure to read labels when you buy paint or colored pencils, avoiding any material that contains lead. Swallowing of any lead-based art materials can lead to brain damage. Be sure that your child is safe from this readily avoidable catastrophe. You should also be aware that so-called "lead" pencils contain not lead but graphite, a form of carbon. It is not recommended that children eat graphite, but it is not harmful in small quantities. Some toddlers who are still struggling with toilet training may wish to avoid the messiness of paints; this is not unusual. There is no rush. Make paints available when you feel the child is ready. Be sure to supply clothes so the child can feel free to move. Because tempera is a water-based paint it washes off easily. Demonstrate this to the child and explain that it is okay to be messy and have fun. Toddlers generally enjoy finger painting, delighting in creating designs with this wonderful, smeary substance. However, I do not encourage older children or adults to use this medium. Finger paints encourage smearing, and while their use is a step forward in art for the toddler, it is a step backward for the older child or adult.

As mentioned earlier, scribbling with the younger child is a step forward in learning how to hold and direct crayons on paper and imitate an adult. It may appear contradictory here to encourage the slightly older child now to use finger paints. The toddler is struggling with the primary issue of learning to control their bodily functions and may or may not be comfortable with being messy. Finger paints, along with tempera paint, provide a way of defining when and with what it is okay to be messy. Art materials are both manageable and compliant, and they can be manipulated to provide more or less control, depending on the age of the child. As the child moves forward, it is important to introduce more intricate art activities such as cutting and pasting, clay modeling and oil painting. Through these creative expressions, children advance by mastering these new media and developing more control.

I like to illustrate the importance of maintaining control by describing an interesting phenomenon that I have observed repeatedly when introducing art therapy concepts to student nurses and medical students. I ask these students to do a free drawing, and provide paper, crayons and colored pencils. Like most adults, these students have not drawn since grade school and feel very intimidated initially. Many of them invariably produce designs by outlining shapes and filling in the outlines. This is something children learn to do early in their school years. Outlining the shapes provides control; filling in is reminiscent of scribbling. The response of these students is understandable. They perceive that I am asking them to do something they consider childish. Discussion of this process is effective in helping these students develop some appreciation for art therapy. If I had offered them finger paints, their perception of being asked to behave in a childish manner would have been stronger. They could not have established their own controls as easily, and I would have done them a disservice by inviting more regression, and perhaps even causing embarrassment.

The child's school environment can be an important factor in creative expression. Children in preschool often learn things more quickly than they do at home because their setting provides the added incentive of doing what the other children are doing. However, in preschool there may also be a shortage of teachers or aides to help the preschooler test new experiences. Both teachers and parents should be aware of each child's progress, assessing whether it is consistent with that of other children and appropriate for the child's age level.

Going to school for the first time should open new vistas for the child who has been encouraged to be creative. New ideas, and perhaps new materials, will be introduced in the classroom and in peer activities. Parents should show an interest in new creative projects and encourage children to continue to create at home. Both parents and teachers should be aware of what children are saying in their art work.

Stimulating creativity in your children requires using your own creative resources. There is no need to buy elaborate art supplies; many things around the house can be used. Bits of fabric, pieces of string or yarn, and old boxes all can be combined in a wonderful variety of ways. Styrofoam egg cartons or paper cups make excellent watercolor pans. Vegetables and sponges can be dipped in paint and used to print interesting designs. All of us who have "made art" with children or worked where there were limited funds for art supplies have learned to improvise with whatever was available. Books purchased or borrowed from the library can help you think of new ideas.

It is not necessary or even important to run out and buy the very best art supplies. It is important to show the child that you are interested in their artwork, no matter what subject matter and no matter what materials have been selected for artistic expression.

Creativity can be expressed through sewing and building as through drawing, and the lessons to be learned can be applied to any form of creative expression as the following examples make clear.

Lynne, age 6, loved to watch her mother sew clothes for her and her sisters. It was obvious that Lynne wanted to be like Mommy by making clothes for her dolls. To encourage this interest, Lynne's mother gave her a toy sewing machine that actually sewed and taught her how to use it. She also showed Lynne where fabric scraps were kept and encouraged her to use these scraps to make her creations. When not in school or playing outside, Lynne would spend hours sewing. After several months a friend asked Lynne's mother to make pillow covers from some very expensive fabric. The fabric was stored temporarily on the "fabric shelf." Lynne, having been told she could take scraps from that shelf, discovered this beautiful fabric and decided to cut it up for a doll's dress. Needless to say, Lynne's mother was horrified, and she panicked when she discovered that the fabric had been cut. How could she handle this situation? She realized that she was responsible because she should have stored the fabric in a different place or explained to Lynne not to use it. To punish the child would have been unfair. Lynne's mother said that she would explain the disaster to her friend. She also acknowledged to Lynne that she had made a mistake, and she asked Lynne to check with her in the future before selecting fabric. She was careful to praise Lynne's creativity and to encourage her to continue sewing, so that this one bad experience would not discourage Lynne from expressing herself in the future. Telling Lynne about the situation demonstrated how people must be responsible for their actions. Showing her how the problem was resolved helped her to learn to take responsibility for her own actions.

Nine-year-old Evan was very involved in "Dungeons and Dragons," a fantasy adventure game. Evan was very talented artistically, creating his own characters and adventures. His father, who enjoyed miniature train sets, decided that he and Evan should build a train platform. Evan did not agree. He wanted to spend the time building a castle for his "Dungeons and Dragons" characters. Evan's father was very disappointed; he thought sharing a creative activity with his son would be a special experience for them both. His basic assumption was correct, but the experience had to be one that interested Evan. Suppressing his own disappointment, the father told Evan that he would be very glad to help with the castle. Together they shopped for necessary supplies, and the father was available whenever Evan heeded help. Evan's mother suggested that space in Evan's bedroom could be used to build the castle, and she offered praise as the project progressed. Evan's younger brother was told that he could watch but not touch. It is not always easy to have our children reject our interests, but Evan's father knew that, in this instance, favoring his son's interests over his own would be more productive.

Evan's story is a good reminder that when you are trying to inspire creative expression in your child that it is the child's interests that should be fostered. Sometimes, unconsciously, adults plan a project or shared art activity that expresses their own wishes, wants, and needs rather than those of the child.

Chapter 3

Babble-Scribble Stage/Sequence

Around 18 Months to 2 1/2 Years

In the preceding chapters, we presented information, posed questions, and gave some answers about what you can learn from children's drawings. We promised that Chapters 4 through 7 would include an in-depth discussion of developmental indicators that can be expressed through children's artistic productions. To help you make this delightful journey through the developmental stages of childhood, we have created twins, Adam and Lisa. We will follow these imaginary siblings as they grow from infancy to age 11. A glimpse at their behavior during these periods of growth will help you to understand how children normally interact with people and objects in their environment and how the proper responses from important adults can stimulate learning. As we travel with the twins and their real-life counterparts, there will be many examples and illustrations to help you recognize these signs of normal growth in creative work produced by children.

The First 18 Months   Adam and Lisa enter the world without any complications, and their parents are glad to know that the children have no physical abnormalities. All the necessary parts are in place and their first cries are strong. Soon after birth, the twins discover their mouths and the pleasure derived from putting something into them. They prefer food, but as the months go by they discover wonderful substitutes—pacifiers, blankets, sleeves of clothing, soft toys, an offered finger from an adult. In these early months the twins learn by instinct. They announce certain discomforts, later identified as "hungry" and "wet," by loud cries for attention. Gradually, the babies learn that the discomforts fade when they are touched, caressed, fed, or when their soiled diapers are changed. This early intelligence is acquired on a sensory level.

Initially the twins are not aware that comforting feelings come as a result of something done by something separate from themselves. Gradually, they come to know that a certain sound signals that relief is on the way. Most likely this sound is Mommy's or Daddy's footsteps when they enter the babies' room. Around 6 months of age, the twins begin to be aware that some things they feel, touch, and hear are not part of themselves. This understanding is known as the beginning of ego development. The ego is not something that we can see or feel, but most of us acknowledge that the "ego" is "self" and that the ego is shaped and formed through interactions with the environment.

About 4 to 6 months, Adam and Lisa learn to turn over and sit up; they may try to pull themselves to their feet by holding on to the bars of the crib or playpen. Boys often achieve these accomplishments a little earlier than girls, but having Adam to copy probably inspires Lisa to develop a little faster. In the past, boys were encouraged to be more active physically, and not too many years ago it was believed that the active baby girl would grow up to be a "tomboy"—not exactly acceptable for a girl. Fortunately, this view is changing among enlightened parents, and Lisa is encouraged to test her arms and legs as much as Adam.

However, children, even identical twins, are not all born alike. Some are naturally more active than others; some are more content to lie quietly and participate in their surroundings by seeing and listening. Adam wants to sit quietly at times, and his parents have learned to match and respond to his movements. This security makes Adam trustful and willing to venture into his small but enlarging world. As Adam and Lisa begin to explore spaces around them, their experience reassures them that someone is there if needed.

Around 8 months, Adam and Lisa become very upset when they are with strangers. This reaction is typical for this age, but by about 14 to 16 months they outgrow it.

The twins begin to walk around 1 year of age, moving their arms and legs more purposefully. They know when to hold on to objects to steady themselves, and the growing strength of their grasp gives them confidence. They discover that a familiar face can disappear and reappear; a ball can roll behind a couch and not be lost forever. In fact, the twins' expanded mobility now makes it possible for them to follow that ball and make it known that they need help to retrieve it. They can also follow Mommy and Daddy into the kitchen, bathroom, and bedroom.

Now that they can grasp more tightly, Adam and Lisa find that feeding themselves is an event. At first they learn by trial and error. They can push the plate, smear food with the spoon, and make something that they do not like disappear by dropping it or throwing it. They also learn that playing with food does not make Mommy or Daddy smile. The twins are discovering new accomplishments and creating new tasks to master. This ongoing process is fundamental to learning.

18 Months to 2 1/2 Years

Adam, age 18 months, is sitting in the sandbox. He picks up a toy, examines it, and discards it for another. He pushes the sand around and watches it fall through his fingers. Occasionally he glances at his twin sister, Lisa, but he is much more interested in his own activity. Lisa puts some sand in her mouth and realizes that it does not taste very good, but this causes another problem—the sand is sticking to her wet fingers and she does not like this feeling. She tries to remove the sand from her fingers by rubbing her hands together. When that is not successful, she uses her shirt, as if it were a towel, to clean off the sand. Giving up the struggle, she reaches for a toy. Her brother's play attracts her attention and she moves swiftly, trying to snatch the bucket he is holding. Adam is very angry and swings the bucket at Lisa. Fortunately, Mommy has been supervising closely. She moves Lisa to another place in the sandbox and gives Lisa another bucket.

Adam and Lisa are behaving like most 18-month-old children. Their attention span is short, and the children are distracted easily. They are not yet ready to share toys or play together, and they are unable to communicate with words. Adam may know a few words, but not enough to tell Lisa what he thinks about her reaching for his toy. He can make his feelings known with body movements, and he can call an adult to rescue him. Both Lisa and Adam will babble to themselves and to others. Their acquisition of language will depend largely on how much they are encouraged to learn words.

Around this same age, the twins are becoming aware that they can resist certain expectations from the adults who care for them. They can master the word "no" and use it so often that this period—and the next 6 months to a year is often referred to as the "negative stage." Parents have called it the "terrible twos." This is a necessary stage—the child is testing limits in an effort to define acceptable behavior and establish independence.

Around age 2, the twins will gradually be faced with either submitting to toilet training or displeasing the adults they have come to trust. Toilet training is a normal battle for control and an important time for Adam and Lisa to learn how far they can go before Mommy and Daddy say "no." Lisa may become toilet trained a little earlier than Adam, which is not unusual. While the development of sphincter control is generally equal in boys and girls, boys usually are slower in complying. Both children will

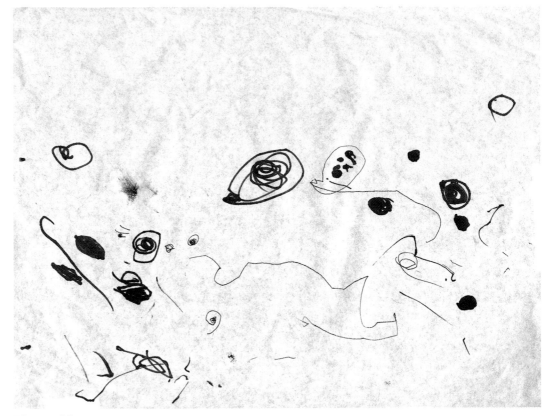

Figure 40

have "accidents" for months and maybe years to come, which also is to be expected.

The twins delight in being given crayons and paper. If they sit close to each other, they will draw on each other's paper. At first they will not be able to stay within the edges of the paper, and they will make marks on any available surface. Someone must watch to make sure that they do not put the crayons in their mouths. By the time the twins are 2, they should enjoy making lines in all directions, interspersing them with dots. The children recognize colors and eventually learn to say the names of these colors, with the help of Mommy and Daddy. With prodding they will name their scribbles, although they probably did not have a particular object in mind when they started to draw.

The following are examples of scribble drawings from the twins' real-life counterparts.

Holly's mother is an artist, and crayons and paper are always available. Holly, at 2, spontaneously produces many scribble pictures (**Fig. 40**).

While Holly's scribbling traveled all over her paper, Hal also 2, preferred to draw separate pictures in different sections of the paper (**Fig. 41**). Hal has just been introduced to paints and, with close supervision, handles them remarkably well for his age.

At 2 years and 10 months, Joey is able to use a crayon in different ways—rapidly and loosely to fill in the area at the top, and more tightly and slowly to create the form at the bottom (**Fig. 42**). When his mother asked him to describe the picture, he said it was "a steam shovel with a man inside."

Figure 41

The way small children progress in handling various art materials tells us how well they are developing fine motor control—the ability to progress from drawing loose random lines with crayons to drawing fine controlled lines with pencils or felt-tipped pens. Some children will develop this fine motor control faster than others.

Child development experts believe that children do not have a plan in mind when they begin to scribble; therefore, we would not expect to be able to detect any danger signals in scribbled images. However, we might have some cause for concern if a child were not interested in "playing" on paper with crayon by age 2. This kind of situation could reflect other developmental delays and should be investigated.

Figure 42

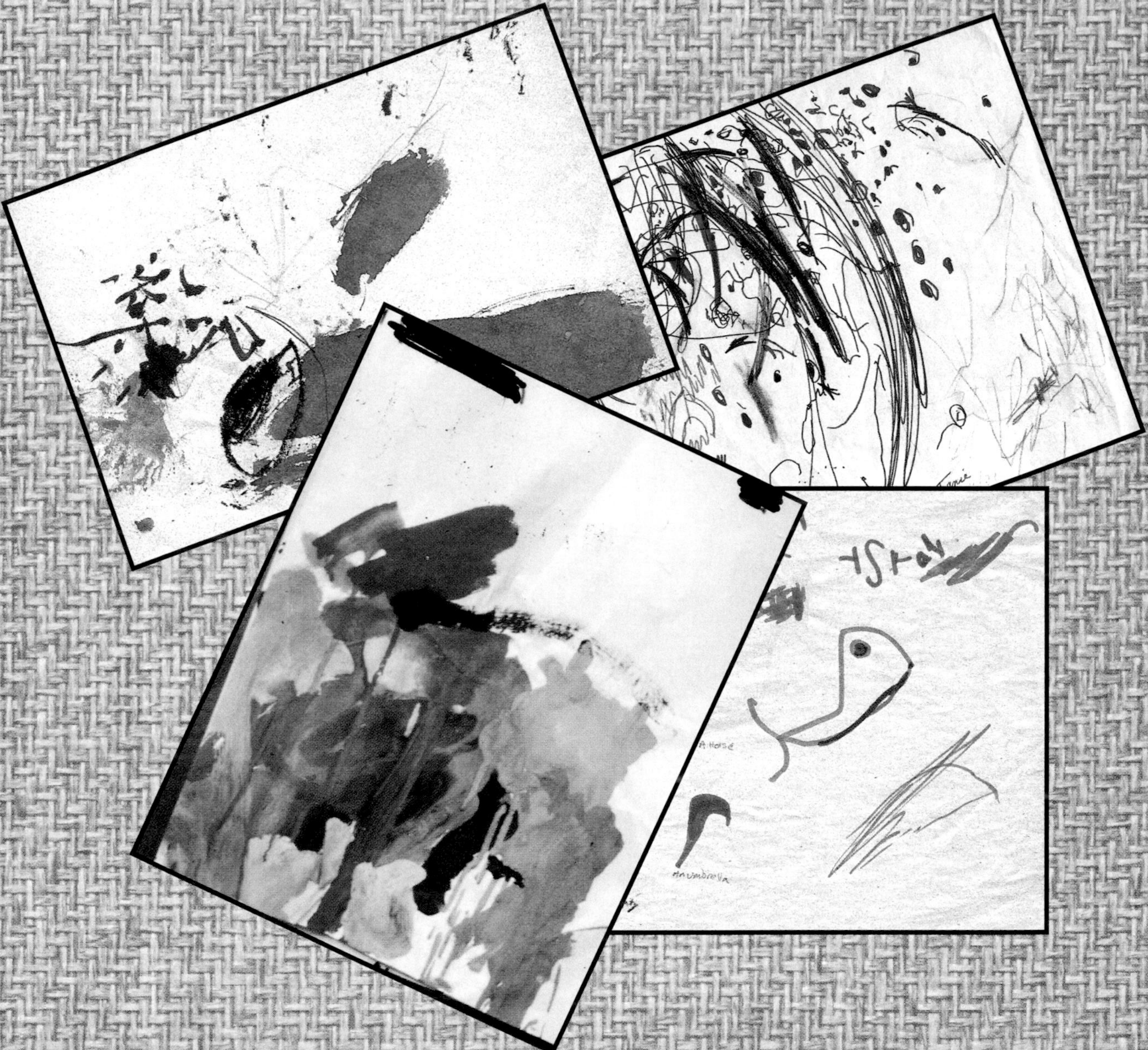
A Horse
An umbrella

Chapter 4

Word-Shape Stage/Sequence

Around 2 1/2 to 4 Years

Adam, 3, is sitting on the floor in his bedroom, playing with miniature cars. With one in each hand, he zooms them around the space in front of him, crashing them into each other at one moment and whizzing them past each other the next. He makes loud noises to accompany the cars' movements and intersperses these sounds with commands to the imaginary drivers. Lisa, his twin sister, is in her bedroom playing with her dollhouse. She is busily rearranging the furniture and telling an imaginary Mommy doll to "hurry and make lunch; the children are hungry."

Around 3, all children start to be interested in specific toys and "play out" activities, imitating parents or other caregivers, stories they have heard, or television programs they have seen. Mimicking special adults in their lives pleases Adam and Lisa greatly. It also helps them to handle uncomfortable feelings that result from disagreements with Mommy or Daddy.

The twins still often play side by side, but not yet with each other. Sharing toys is still difficult and may need mediating—Adam and Lisa do not want to share any of their possessions. This proprietary attitude extends to their beds, special plates, and eating utensils. Certain blankets and bedtime companions, such as a teddy bear or doll, become important objects in their world. In the normal transition period, in which children give up some of their attachment to Mommy, Daddy, or early caregivers, these personal claims are necessary substitutes helping them in the natural process of becoming separate from these adults.

During the word-shape stage/sequence, words are repeated for pleasure at first. Gradually they are connected and take on more meaning. Adam and Lisa speak in monologues to themselves. Even when stimulated by a question or command from another child or an adult, the response still sounds like a monologue, unrelated to the question or command. At this age words are clear, but complete sentences are more the exception than the rule. Adam and Lisa will learn more about words and sentences by example from their parents and other adults, but they will still continue their monologues for a while. They cannot be expected to hold conversations before they are ready. These skills will be accomplished at each child's own pace.

By age 3, the twins are aware of themselves as separate persons and will assert themselves frequently to confirm their place in the household. Only in the past few months have they felt very comfortable playing in a room by themselves; they still leave their play frequently to make sure that a special adult is nearby. Mealtimes are less messy, but the struggle over toilet training has not been resolved. By definite words and actions, Adam and Lisa demonstrate that they will decide to regulate their bowel and bladder habits when they are ready. Their preoccupation with this process is often reflected in their going out of their way to avoid unpleasant odors. This will probably stop when they are more willing to comply with adult requests.

Adam and Lisa delight in walking, running, and handling new objects, but their movements are not always smooth. The twins run around the house excitedly, sometimes bumping into furniture and breaking things. Like other 3- to 4-year-old children, they do not always want to admit they are responsible for the damage. They blame another child or create an imaginary friend or animal to be the target for the ensuing reprimand. When they grow to understand that someone can be angry with them but still love them, the necessity to blame imaginary friends dwindles. However, these imaginary friends may continue to serve as playmates until the child goes to school.

Early in this stage/sequence, scribbling is still evident in the twins' drawings, but gradually certain shapes will emerge and forms are outlined. The children begin to organize forms on paper, and they show an early sense of balance by drawing both large and small shapes. They combine some of these forms to look like recognizable objects, although the shape may be primitive and somewhat abstract. The world in which children live influence the objects crudely symbolized in their drawings and clay sculptures. They particularly enjoy rolling clay into long strips and round patties and drawing shapes they will tell you are monsters. Adam may master the scribble more quickly than Lisa, but within the year, like most children their age, their skills will be similar.

Here are some word-shape pictures created by the twins real-life counterparts at this age.

When Nicole is 2, her mother shows her how to use paint. Together they create a picture Nicole calls "Crickets" **(Fig. 43)**. Paint is a new experience for Nicole at this age. Nicole's mother tells us that Nicole has been delighted with the "smeary" quality, but she has needed help to keep the paint on the paper.

Jamie is just past 3 when she produces this drawing with colored felt-tipped pens **(Fig. 44)**. Jamie's parents furnish her with a rich array of art supplies, and she spends much time experimenting with them. In this picture she scribbles, draws forms inside other forms, and adds some lines. Notice how she is able to stay within the boundaries of the paper, considering the many images she wants to create.

Figure 43

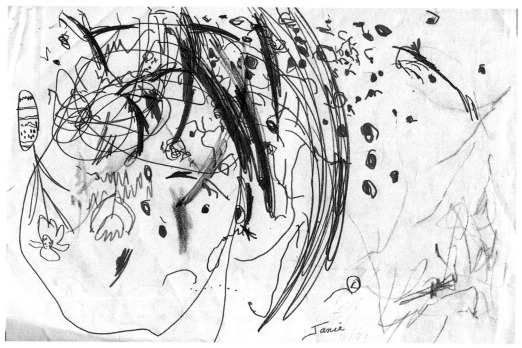

Figure 44

Figure 45

It was a joy to meet Tony, who attended a preschool where I was known as the "art lady." Tony was one of the most self-sufficient 3-year-old children I have ever met. Like Hal, he spent most of his free time drawing or painting. During my four weeks at the school, Tony invited me to look at his drawings or draw with him whenever I was free. The children worked on easels, and it was not easy to control dripping paint. Tony has discovered that he can make interesting designs from these "accidents" and has begun to create them consciously **(Fig. 45)**. This is a remarkable accomplishment for a 3-year-old child. Tony's rapid advancement in artistic development was demonstrated in two other situations.

One morning Tony asked me to sit with him while he drew with colored chalk on a small chalkboard. He wanted to produce a tree, grass, and sun, and he asked me to help him with these images. I took another chalkboard and in a simplistic way illustrated these objects, suggesting that Tony try to copy them on his chalkboard. I was not surprised that he was able to do this successfully. I was surprised a week later, however, when he greeted me with a detailed chalk drawing of these same objects. He was delighted that he had been able to replicate a picture that had been erased the previous week.

Tony's capacity to recall the instruction he had received and reproduce the objects so well over a period of eight days reinforced my impression that he was a very bright child who functioned on a more advanced level than most 3-year-old children. Imitating my drawing suggested that Tony was also beginning to seek out adults he wanted to imitate. This behavior usually occurs closer to 4 or 5 years of age. The preschool staff reported that Tony was advanced in all areas of cognitive and emotional development, supporting my perceptions gleaned from his creative expressions.

Holly, at 3, combines shapes and lines to produce "a man with funny hair" **(Fig. 46)**. The familiar scribble and her description of the picture focus our attention on the top of the head. Children this age typically emphasize the head. Developmental psychologists believe that the rapid physical growth experienced by all children between birth and 4 or 5 years creates a feeling of imbalance in the child. Efforts to master this feeling, probably first expressed by drawing large and small shapes are now reflected by placing unrealistically large objects on the top of the head, by making one limb larger than the other, or by exaggerating the size of hands and feet. Holly's aware-

Figure 46

ness of the opposite sex is also emerging—a natural course of events for children this age. There are two important men in her life, her father and her older brother, so it is no surprise that she calls this figure a "man."

Warning Signals at 3

The most significant warning signal at this age would be continuous scribbling with no evidence that the child is able to outline shapes within the scribbles or produce spontaneous combinations of shapes and lines. It would also be important to note whether the child is advancing from babbling to saying words and incomplete sentences. These two developmental progressions generally occur at about the same time, and the strong presence or absence of advancing language or drawing skills are cause for concern.

In Chapter 2 we introduced Indira, the little girl from India who created the same images in paint as her Western playmates. "Doing art" with me at her preschool, Indira was very intrigued with colors and typically used them in a way that pleased her but had little to do with the actual color of an object. One day in particular, she had been using a variety of colored markers to draw forms that she named (**Fig. 47**). Indira called the large yellow shape a "horse," the turquoise form a "cat," and the orange figure an "umbrella." Between these images she drew some scribbles, but told me they were "nothing." Finally she picked up a pencil and drew a very light form in the lower left corner. She said this was "Mr. Uppity." This child's choice of pencil to draw a human form was as surprising as her name for this barely visible figure. She had made this image distinctly separate from the others—it had no color and was a human instead of an animal or inanimate object. She would not tell me anything about "Mr. Uppity," and I would not press her to discuss it. It was obvious, however, that it symbol-

Figure 47

ized something or someone that did not deserve the colorful attention she gave the other images. I later learned Indira was familiar with a popular children's book containing a character called Mr. Uppity. I realized that Indira was sufficiently influenced by this character to reflect her response in a drawing.

Subsequently, my experience in assessing children's drawings led me to query the preschool staff about Indira's behavior. I asked whether she handled distress situations by withdrawing. The teachers reported that when Indira was asked to do something she did not want to do, was having difficulty with another child, or was overly tired, she did not express her feelings, although she had a good command of English. She would either remove herself physically from the situation or have a temper tantrum so a member of the staff would be compelled to take her aside. We discussed the possibility that "Mr. Uppity" symbolized Indira's feelings of separateness in an environment where she was a minority. We also discussed the fact that she was the youngest of five children and perhaps was treated in an infantile way at home, making it more difficult for her to handle the usual demands of preschool. We all agreed that more communication between Indira's family and the preschool staff would ease this 3 1/2-year-old girl's transition from home to school, so that she would be less likely to choose infantile ways to remove herself from challenging situations.

As Adam and Lisa move into the fourth year of their lives, they will face new experiences that will help them grow and learn new skills. These experiences and the new challenges they bring will be discussed in the next chapter.

Chapter 5

Sentence-Picture Stage/Sequence

Around 4 To 7 Years

4 Years

Adam, 4, sits on the living room floor, playing with the life-like female doll he had requested the previous Christmas. He is "Mommy," spanking his baby brother for "not drinking his bottle." Meanwhile, Adam's twin sister, Lisa, is busy in an upstairs bedroom. Preening before a full-length mirror in her mother's out-of-style clothes, she relays instructions to an imaginary babysitter. The beaded dress droops in folds around Lisa's ankles and trails on the floor; a large, floppy hat nearly covers her small, round face, completely hiding half of her head and all of her hair.

Four-year-old Lisa, like all children her age, is preoccupied with her own interests. She imitates Mommy and other important women in her life, pretending to cook and clean if Mommy is a homemaker, playing dentist if Mommy is a dentist, and "dressing up" like Mommy. Hair styles, makeup, and clothes are fun if they are also important to "Mommy" or a "Mommy" figure.

More than likely, Lisa has mastered her bodily functions and is quite pleased with herself. The adults around her are pleased, too. Naturally, there are times when Lisa does not like her interactions with Mommy. For example, if Mommy is too busy caring for a new baby brother to give Lisa the amount of attention Lisa wants, it might not be such fun to dress up and care for dolls. Lisa might be more likely to spank the doll, or throw the "bad" doll into a corner.

Whether or not children are able to act out their feelings, they may want to put some of these feelings into their drawings. They may even demand that these productions be displayed on the family showcase—the refrigerator door. This can also happen in the preschool or day care center where the teacher or aide represents a mother figure. The 4-year-old girl will have fun imitating Teacher, too, and sometimes be displeased with Teacher because of real or imagined slights. It takes some time to conquer the feelings that accompany being separated for a long stretch of the day from Mommy. Lisa may express her thoughts and feelings about this new experience in destructive play, and/or on her drawings.

Adam, like all boys his age, is still strongly attached to Mommy. He will be 5 or 6 before he begins to imitate Daddy. Now, however, it is not unusual for Adam to imitate Mommy in the same ways Lisa does: playing with dolls, doing housework, or playing dentist. Adam's feelings of jealousy about a baby brother will be similar to Lisa's. Adam, too, may resent being taken to a day-care center or left with a sitter. We said before that boys are slower in learning to control bodily functions, and Adam may still be struggling with this developmental task.

Like Lisa, Adam will express feelings through play and drawings. He and Lisa will learn that destructive play results in punishment. Learning this is important, because during this period in their young lives Adam and Lisa begin to understand right and wrong. They learn what is acceptable social behavior, what makes those large, powerful adults around them angry and/or happy. At the same time, Adam and Lisa realize that drawing or painting their feelings and thoughts remains an acceptable and rewarding activity. They know these "creations" are not always understood by those same large and powerful adults, but these adults are always pleased with the children's art work. The more Adam and Lisa learn to behave like Mommy, Daddy, and teacher, the more they will tell us in their drawings how they feel about limits and expectations.

During this stage of their growth, Adam and Lisa develop a greater awareness of objects around them. They now can produce recognizable images, even when such images—a bed, for example—are out of sight. At first they will draw only one object at a time. Gradually, Adam and Lisa will begin to draw several objects on the same page. These objects may have no realistic relationship to each other. The door on Adam's house may be too small to walk through for the person he has drawn on the same page. The flower in Lisa's drawing may be larger than the person she draws on the same page.

Depending on the kind of stimulation they receive at home and at school, at this age Adam and Lisa may begin to read words and learn to converse socially. Speech continues to be a monologue, but it is now interspersed with attempts to be understood by others. Intellectual skills naturally improve with age, making the twins' verbal responses to others more appropriate. They understand and can offer criticism, commands, requests, and threats. As the social need to communicate verbally increases, Lisa and Adam will learn more ways to speak with others.

The following drawings were produced by real-life children the same age as Lisa and Adam.

We met Scott briefly in Chapter 1 (**Fig. 28**). Let us look a little more closely at this image produced when Scott is 4. The scribbles and shapes within shapes are joined to represent a figure. One big circle is the head and two little circles inside are just where the eyes belong. A line marks the mouth. Scott knows that there are arms, legs, hands, and feet, and he connects them to the head. It looks as though he was trying to scribble hair but did not quite connect it to the top of the head. It does not matter that the hair does not quite connect, or that there is no body and nose. What does matter is that Scott is beginning to put together the artistic skills he had mastered over the previous 2 1/2 years, to make something that even adults can recognize as a human figure. This drawing represents a classical developmental image that psychologists call a "tadpole" figure.

Dayna, also 4, is still mastering the word-shape stage, drawing shapes within shapes and beginning to connect them to represent a figure, all within the same picture (**Fig. 11**). Dayna is still drawing some of the images that gave her pleasure in the not-too-distant past. The embracing of these images is much the same as Linus's need (in the "Peanuts" cartoon) to carry a security blanket everywhere he goes. However, emerging from these early images is a figure that now includes a head similar to the one in Scott's drawing (**Fig. 28**). Dayna's drawing of the head includes a nose. She has made another circle for the body and added arms and legs.

Dayna, the third child in her family, has two older sisters and a baby brother. Both parents have careers outside the home. Dayna's mother is an artist who encourages her children to express themselves freely with a variety of art materials. The children have no known developmental problems. An older sibling is naturally a model to copy, and a new baby in the house, who receives much attention, arouses a wish within Dayna to be a baby again. These normal mixed emotions are expressed in the blending of stages and sequences and the transition from one period of growth to another within one drawing. Later you will see other creative drawings from Dayna and her sisters.

Keith, 4, enjoyed attending preschool. He was not interested in learning to read, much preferring to have someone read to him from his older brother's books. Keith did love to draw, however, and he received an abundance of drawing materials from his parents, teacher, and artist grandmother. For an art activity at preschool, Keith was asked to depict "Spring" (Fig. 48). He has no problem pasting bits of colored paper to represent the foliage of a tree, and he has drawn lines down under the colorful collage to create the trunk. The image is bright and cheerful, reflecting Keith's bright and cheerful feeling about spring and the art activity. It is no surprise that the colors he chose are not realistic. Children of this age more often select colors they like, paying little attention to the actual color of an object.

At age 4 years, 7 months, Keith has been able to draw a picture with more than one object (Fig. 49). On the same piece of paper he has drawn a house, a tree, a sun, clouds, and rain. Typically at this age, houses can be taller than trees; sun and rain can be present at the same time. Keith tells us that he now knows these elements in his environment and is able to represent them in a recognizable way.

Figure 48   Figure 49

Houses, suns, and trees appear frequently in children's drawings. The houses often represent security and warmth. Suns and trees represent powerful objects in the environment. A tree may also represent self. In Keith's drawing these three objects symbolize the three most important objects in his young life—his mother, his father, and himself.

Lilly, 4 years, 2 months, has painted a family portrait— mother, father, and child (**Fig. 50**). Lilly's father is a colleague of mine, and Lilly drew many pictures that were used as examples in art therapy classes. Although Lilly has an older sister, the sister does not appear in this painting. Lilly is just learning to deal with Mother and Father as two separate people, but she is not ready to include her older sister in any "family" portrait. She solves her problem in a wonderful way, simply by omitting her sister from the painting—a natural solution at Lilly's age.

Around the same time, Lilly uses crayons to draw a house, a sun and a lamp on a table. In this picture (**Fig. 51**) Lilly substitutes a lamp for the symbolic tree. Like normal 4-year-old children, Lilly is telling us symbolically which objects are important in her life at this time. Lilly drew the lamp on the table outside of the house on the same page. She drew a face on the sun. Placing interiors and exteriors side by side, and faces on suns are not unusual images at 4.

Figure 50

Figure 51

These two examples of Lilly's creativity illustrate her ability to handle crayon and paint and to represent objects graphically somewhat better than most children her age. This could be attributed to the fact that in addition to her natural talent, drawing and painting are encouraged and rewarded. Lilly knows that her art work is often presented to college students who are learning to be art therapists.

Hal, at 4, has discovered "King Kong" (**Fig. 52**). He combines his mastery of the scribble, lines, and shapes to create an image of this monstrous gorilla towering over many other forms, some more recognizable than others. Hal is trying to tell a story and make some order out of his impressions of someone else's fantasy—one that could be frightening to any child of 4. We do not know that Hal was frightened, but we do know that he wants to show us some of his thoughts and feelings about "King Kong." Hal's artistic and cognitive skills are not far enough advanced at this age to make the story very clear. His control of the art materials and efforts to communicate so many details in one picture are more likely to occur at 5 years of age than at 4. We said before that Hal was encouraged at a very early age to experiment with different art materials, and his innate abilities have helped him to learn more quickly than most children.

Ray, 4, who lives across the country from Hal, also is impressed with "King Kong" and has drawn the monster hovering over a "boat, fish and lobster" (**Fig. 53**). Like Hal, Ray too is trying to tell a story about this gigantic creature, much bigger than all the other objects in the drawing. Ray's forms are not connected in a logical, coherent fashion and they are not expected to be at age 4.

We have mentioned that children around 4 years of age are naturally learning to deal with Mommy and Daddy, and specific caregivers. Many of their pictures around this time include three objects—usually parents and child, or house, tree, and sun. Ray's representation of this important threesome includes Daddy and two other members of the family "in the woods." He has used the familiar scribble appropriately to fill in the bodies, hair, and ground. Ray's mastery of shapes within shapes has led to the creation of eyes and mouths. We believe he is expressing personal feelings and thoughts about two of the figures by placing them so close to each other but separate from

Figure 52

Figure 53

the third form **(Fig. 54)**. Had we asked, he might have told us why he did that, but this really is not necessary. Ray has invested much energy and time in creating a colorful picture, and once he has finished it, he is eager to move on to some other activity.

The drawings by Hal and Ray of "King Kong," and Ray's picture of the three family members (excluding himself), are examples of how children begin to express on paper strong impressions from the world around them. In the process, they master the feelings and thoughts stimulated by these people and events.

Figure 54

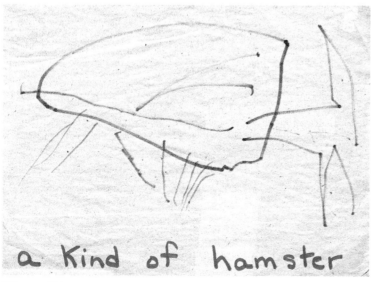

Figure 55

Warning Signals at 4

I met Leon when he was 4 years, 1 month old. He was a delightful, stocky boy, who was very articulate for his age and played nicely with the other children in the preschool. It was surprising, therefore, to see his drawings. Most of the time he produced line drawings more typical of a 2- or 3-year-old child than a 4-year-old. One day he outlined a shape, extending lines from it, and told me it was "a kind of hamster" **(Fig. 55)**. I was struck by the fact that he seemed to be aware that it was not an adequate image of a hamster. There was an inconsistency in his behavior, which appeared normal for his age, and his artistic development, which reflected a lower level of intellectual and emotional development. This observation led me to gather more information about Leon. I learned that Leon had been hospitalized several times during the previous year for serious ear problems. Illness and hospitalizations that interrupt the normal developmental process can cause what psychologists call "developmental lags." Leon was not showing signs of regression, that is, going back to a previous level of development. Rather, he was telling us that he was still a little behind the other children in some areas of maturity.

In a previous chapter we discussed Bobby, who was drawing "gaping mouths" on all of the faces of figures. Aside from this one unusual repeated image, his images were varied and similar to those of other children his age. One of those forms, unnamed, is very similar to Leon's "kind of a hamster" (**Fig. 56**). This picture had been made by Bobby at 3 years 4 months of age—almost a year younger than Leon when he produced **Fig. 55.** This drawing is normal for Bobby's age, but comparing these two drawings will help you to understand what we mean when we say Leon is creating images on an earlier developmental level. Almost a year younger than Leon, Bobby is easily drawing a form that is still difficult for Leon.

A lag in development is not unusual for a child who has experienced repeated hospitalizations within a year. This development was not observable in play, but it certainly would have been apparent when Leon started school. He was showing us through his art that he needed more support and encouragement than his peers, to help him make up for lost time.

The painting that Harry, 4, made in preschool, I refer to as a "muddy blob" (**Fig. 57**). As I watched, Harry applied one color on top of another, smearing it all together, like a 2- or 3-year-old child who has just discovered paint. A few weeks later, I observed Harry drawing circles with a pencil and trying to fill them in with orange paint. In the first picture, Harry was regressing—returning to an earlier level of development. We know that because Harry's second picture tells us that he is very capable of drawing circles with a pencil and controlling paint. These two very different images within a period of several weeks signal us to explore Harry's world further. How does he behave? Is there anything about his home environment that might explain this erratic creative expression? In Harry's case we were able to learn some answers.

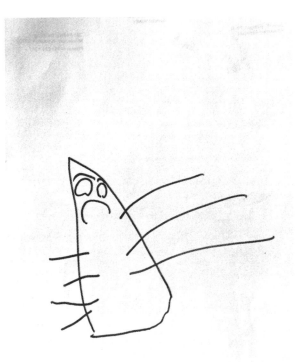

Figure 56

Figure 57

Like his drawings, Harry's behavior in school and at home was erratic. Sometimes he would act like an extremely mature 4-year-old. At other times he would whine, cling to his mother (at home), or the preschool teacher and reject the attentions of any other staff person. The director of the institution in which this particular preschool was housed shed some light on Harry's problems. This little boy's mother was expecting another child in a few months. Mother and father were a bright, intelligent, and sophisticated couple. They lovingly believed that sharing the process of the pregnancy would help Harry accept the new baby more easily. Sharing meant inviting Harry to touch and see Mother's growing body and to give him information about the birth process.

Harry's parents meant well in trying to share the details of his sibling's birth, but this kind of information is too much for any 4-year-old to handle. Harry's drawings and behavior told us he vacillated between the need to regress—smearing paint and clinging to home and school "Mommies"—and the need to try to control his anxieties by drawing circles to contain paint or by acting like an adult. Many of us believe that if we are "open" with our children and tell them "everything they need to know," they will grow up without fear of sexuality and will display mature sexual behavior. I believe this is true, but we must also be sensitive to the fact that children will ask questions, especially about birth and sex, when they are ready. Giving too much information too soon, and inviting a 4-year-old boy to touch his mother's growing abdomen and breasts at a time when he is naturally struggling to be like Daddy, can only cause confusion and anxiety. At this age all little boys are still emotionally attached to their mothers (more will be said about this later), and this kind of intimacy can only create havoc, which Harry was manifesting in many ways.

Color pencil drawing by Katie, age 9

Michael, 4 years, ten months, also attended this preschool. I was asked to do an art evaluation. How this came about, the results, and follow up will be discussed in depth in a later chapter. Two drawings clearly indicated difficulty with learning of a perceptual problem (**Figs. 58, 59**). We knew that Michael was showing signs of emotional problems as well. A picture of his family told us a little about some of his sad and angry feelings, and how he was coping with them. This drawing (**Fig. 60**), was produced several days after Michael's evaluation. By this time he was very comfortable working with me and was more than willing to draw his family. At the bottom of the picture, he has drawn what appears to be a fence, and a figure, which he describes as himself "shooting and killing robots with my ray gun." The second figure is his brother, Tom, who is not shooting because "the robot is his best friend." He has identified the third figure as his father who is "not seeing" and "not shooting." When asked, Michael said that mother was not in the picture because "she would get hurt."

Figure 58

Figure 59

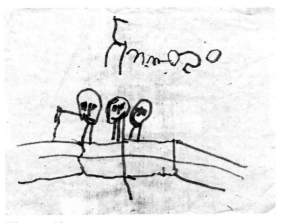

Figure 60

Michael's parents had been separated for a year, and his picture probably represents some of the loss Michael feels about his father's absence from the home. Although there had been no contact between them for a year, Michael wanted his father in the picture. As in a dream, Michael has reversed events. He cannot see his father, so he draws him as someone who is present but "not seeing." Children this age cannot understand the concepts of divorce or separation on an adult level. Michael feels he must explain the loss to himself in some way. Like other children in such a situation, Michael is angry. Some children turn this anger on themselves and decide they are responsible for a parent's "leaving"; some children blame the remaining parent. I suspect that Michael is very angry with his mother and may even fantasize about killing her—feelings and thoughts that he has learned must be suppressed. The drawing is Michael's creation. He is the only person doing the shooting and he has decided to leave Mother out of the scene so she would not get hurt. In Michael's cast of characters, he is the only one who could hurt her.

Michael's drawings and behavior give us an idea of the extent of his difficulties in trying to create order in a disordered household. This effort is made even more difficult for him because of his perceptual problem. As we studied his drawings more closely, we gained some direction to help us plan intervention and treatment for Michael and his family.

5 Years

Around age 5, Adam and Lisa begin to respond differently to Mommy and Daddy. They also have become more aware of the differences between girls and boys.

Lisa still wants Mommy's and Teacher's attention, but now seeks more attention from Daddy—the same kind of attention she sees him giving to Mommy. The pervasive intrusion of television has speeded up the awareness of male-female interactions for Lisa and her twin brother. Lisa is beginning to "flirt" with Daddy and other adult male family friends and relatives.

Adam, on the other hand, not only wants Mommy's attention, but wants to treat her the way he sees Daddy treating her. Traditionally, this would have meant wanting to climb into bed with her and imitating his father by asserting himself around the house. But times are changing for the 4-year-old Adams of the world. They still want to be physically close to Mommy, but the familiar male "macho" image is not necessarily the norm. Adam may enjoy sharing the quiche with both Mommy and Daddy and playing catch with Mommy.

Play activities with other children provide an opportunity for 5-year-olds to act out some of their fantasies about adult relationships, and it is around now that Adam and Lisa will play "house," or pretend to be a doctor, salesman, or carpenter with each other and with other children. An interest in "war games" becomes evident. While in the past this scenario was strictly for the boys, Lisa and her girlfriends now will participate frequently.

Images of people are drawn a little more realistically at age 5, and telling a story in a picture is evidence of better organization of thoughts. This story-telling is aided by the natural advancement of intellectual and artistic skills. These normal accomplishments will appear when Adam and Lisa have mastered all the artistic skills they have learned up to now, which may occur at different times for them and some of their real-life counterparts.

Figure 61

The following drawings were created by 5-year-old boys and girls. You have already seen drawings done by some of these children at an earlier age; it is interesting and valuable to follow their developmental paths through their drawings.

At age 5, Keith attended Sunday school regularly, describing to his parents what he was learning about the creation of the Earth. To reinforce their lessons, Keith and his classmates were asked to draw the seven days of creation. To illustrate day six, Keith drew the creation of Eve from Adam's rib (**Fig. 61**). Adam is definitely bigger than Eve— his hair goes up. Eve's hair goes down. We have also seen some of Keith's drawings at age 4 (**Figs. 48, 49**).

Male-female differences become more explicit at age 5. Even though Keith has omitted hands, feet, and facial features, he has communicated his growing awareness of the differences between Mommy and Daddy by drawing Adam, with short hair, larger than Eve, with long hair—just like his Mommy and Daddy.

In this project Keith has learned that on the seventh day "God rested," and with the typical 5-year-old's ability to understand this and represent it, he has drawn a figure sleeping in bed (**Fig. 62**). In Keith's world, bed is a logical place for resting.

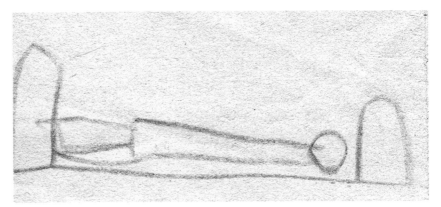

Figure 62

Figure 63

At home Keith often turns to ever available art media. One day he learned that trying to make a tree with paint was not as easy as he thought it would be—paint was messier than crayon. Keith persevered, however, and has created a recognizable tree with surprisingly realistic colors (**Fig. 63**). At age 5, the bottom of the paper is the most obvious base line, and the way Keith has spread his tree over almost all of the paper tells us he does not feel inhibited about expressing himself artistically. This is also true of Keith's verbal communications.

Nicole, also 5, is the daughter of an art therapist mother and a photographer father. She always has free access to all kinds of art materials. Nicole has just acquired her first bicycle, for which Daddy has bought a bell and streamers. She and her father have gone bike riding together, and she has drawn a picture to commemorate this exciting event (**Fig. 64**). We said above that little girls at this age want to be with their fathers, and Nicole is no exception. She appears complete, at the top of the picture, but is much smaller than Daddy on his bicycle. Nicole's mother has unusually long legs, and it probably is not a coincidence that Nicole and Daddy both have unusually long legs in the drawing. She is still combining characteristics of both parents in her drawings.

Figures in profile are not usually seen in the artwork of 5-year-old children, but the open invitation to draw in Nicole's home and her exposure to photography has made her more expressive than most children her age. It has also made her aware that she can recall and record a special time on paper.

Figure 64

Previously, we discussed Scott's progressing recognition of the differences between girls and boys and his ability at age 5 to put more than one object in the same picture.

Figure 65

At the same age, Scott has drawn a boy, a girl, and rainbows **(Fig. 65)**. Scott at 5 wants to be Mommy's little boy as much as he wants to be like Daddy, so the figures represent the important people in his life as well as himself. There is now a new baby sister in the family. We do not know whether the girl in this picture is supposed to represent Mommy or Baby Sister, but she is easily identified as female. The two figures are the same size and Scott is telling us some important thoughts he is having at this time. If he has drawn the girl to represent Mommy, she is now small like Scott; if the girl is a representation of his new sister, she is now big like him and does not need Mommy's undivided attention. While we know Scott naturally wants to be close to Mommy, he draws the boy leaning away from the female figure, but looking at her; at the same time he shows this female figure looking away from him. Mommy and sister are the two females in Scott's life and by representing both in one ambiguous figure he is beginning to realize that it is time to move away from Mommy and accept his sister.

Like most children, Scott is fascinated with rainbows. He has learned about them from stories, and there are three rainbows in his picture. We said previously that one of the ways a child symbolizes a mother/father/child relationship is through three related objects in a drawing. Scott's rainbows may be a way of keeping his "threesome" separate from the "foursome" that now makes up his family.

Children learn about clowns from stories from television or from a trip to the circus. Scott drew a "clown and a boy bouncing balls together" **(Fig. 66)**. The figure of the clown is complete; the figure of the boy is not. Clowns are awesome—they do all kinds of amazing tricks that make children laugh and cry and even feel scared. For children this age, Daddies can also be awesome, especially when little boys are trying to be like them. Scott tells us in this drawing that the little boy (Scott) can "bounce balls" with the clown, but he is not as complete as the clown (Daddy).

Scott's rainbow drawing and clown drawing are personal expressions of his normal developmental efforts to master moving away from Mommy and identifying with Daddy.

Around this time, Scott has drawn a picture that illustrates how children create images that are indicative of past and present sequences of artistic development. Scott wanted to draw a turkey, which is not an easy bird to represent on paper. His effort was a return to combining shapes within

Figure 66

Figure 67

shapes and scribbling to fill in the turkey's body (**Fig. 67**). It is common for a child to try to draw something before he/she has acquired the skills to produce it, especially if, like Scott, he or she is interested in everything in the environment and encouraged to use art media to give expression to these objects.

We discussed Dayna's drawing at age 4 (**Fig. 11**). Becca, Dayna's next older sister, at age 5, has drawn a smiling little girl apparently skipping through the flowers (**Fig. 68**). The large head on the figure and the omission of arms are not unusual at this age. Human beings experience a greater amount of physical growth between birth and 5 to 6 years of age than during any other five-year span of life. This enormous growth spurt stimulates a natural striving for physical balance that is likely to be reflected in children's drawings around this time. Up to around age 7, it is normal to see figures drawn with one leg or arm larger than the other, heads bigger than bodies, big hats and bows on tops of heads, and even the omission of some parts of the body. This would be abnormal if we had other evidence that the child was well past this stage/sequence and capable of drawing people and objects with realistic proportions.

Figure 68

Figure 69

The next three drawings discussed are good examples of images produced by normal 5-year-old children, and show different manifestations of a striving for physical balance.

A teacher gave us Tom's drawing; we know nothing about him other than his age. In this wonderful picture, Tom clearly distinguishes male from female, but he has drawn an oversized head on one figure and unequal arms and legs on both figures. He has used the same lines for hands and feet (**Fig. 69**). It is very interesting to us that he makes the female larger but gives the male a more "aggressive" image. This probably reflects the normal process of this period—Tom is beginning to identify with the important male figure in his life and become less dependent on "Mommy."

Cleo, 5, presents us with a delightful example of "balancing" her female form, and probably some of her thoughts and feelings about being like the special adult female in her life. A hat with an extended ornament sits atop the oversized head. Arms hang down almost to the ankles and legs are longer than the upper portion of the torso. There is no sign of the lower torso. Colors are used unrealistically, and Cleo skillfully combined familiar shapes within shapes, scribbles, and lines. Her "lady" reached from the top to the bottom of the paper (**Fig. 70**). It is apparent that Cleo is having no problems expressing herself artistically.

Figure 70

Figure 71

Some children will move into the story-telling sequence sooner than others. Martin, 5, is telling us about a character who is sitting on top of a large form, and brandishing weapons (**Fig. 71**). (The two rectangular scribbled forms to the left of his head are not part of his story. They were inserted to cover his real name, which was printed very well for his age.) Martin has put what looks like a hat on the head, made one arm larger than the other, and even made the weapons consistent with the size of the arms. The legs are almost hidden, but Martin is showing us his wish and natural need to begin to assert himself.

Warning Signals at 5

We have already presented some examples of warning signals at age 4. In Chapter 8 we will discuss examples of drawings produced by children who were expressing many problems and how their images provided information for determining interventions. Below is further elaboration on an image discussed briefly in the Introduction.

This is Kim's floating house (**Fig. 1**). At 5 1/2 years of age, Kim has drawn a house similar to the houses drawn by other children of that age. However, children at 5 do not usually draw houses floating in air. If not yet able to draw a ground line, a child will use the bottom of the page as a base line, as Keith did. Regardless of the country or climate in which they live, children learn from storybooks that houses often have chimneys, and they will show this in their drawings. Frequently there is even smoke coming from the chimney. Also by 5 1/2, children are normally interested in representing people, making some early distinctions between female and male. You have seen an example of this. Intellectually they are able, also, to put more than one object in a picture.

Kim's drawing has none of these normal indicators. A professional art therapist's view of the images in Kim's drawing raises questions about his home life. Who cares for him? What are his relationships with these care-givers? Why does the picture make the therapist feel that Kim is lonely, isolated, and depressed? And, finally, how does the drawing reflect Kim's behavior in preschool?

What we learned was that Kim lived in an orphanage in Eastern Europe until the age of 3, when he was adopted by a couple from a Western European country and brought to a land that was new to him. Both countries, incidentally, experience all four seasons, and houses heated by fireplaces are more the rule than the exception. When Kim showed signs of difficulty in adjusting to his new environment, his adoptive parents had him psychologically tested, and I met him while he was attending preschool.

Kim could not play with the other children and rarely paid attention to group activities, although his command of the new language was more than adequate. He saw a psychotherapist once a week and a volunteer aide in the preschool stayed with him constantly. It was believed that, based on his history, he needed one person to relate to, and trust, before he could make relationships with other staff and children.

I relate an experience that typifies Kim's abnormal behavior. I had been at the school every day for several weeks, and while Kim kept his usual distance from me, I was not a "stranger"; he knew me by name. Kim was playing alone in the sandbox when I approached quietly and asked if I could watch him play. He became very excited and told me I had to turn my back and stay that way until he was finished. I could not see what he was making until he gave me permission. I did as he requested, turning around only when he said it was okay. I admired the form Kim had created from the sand and asked him to tell me something about it. He acknowledged my praise, but he would not talk to me and would not look me in the eye. All of this behavior is abnormal for a child of this age.

I learned also that Kim was not encouraged to draw at school, either alone or with the other children. His therapist told me that his mother frequently made him draw at home and was often critical of his drawings. The teachers and preschool staff naturally wanted to avoid creating this same kind of stress. I asked to see what Kim would express through his drawings. It was decided that while playing "house" with him in the kitchen, the aide would hand Kim some paper and felt-tipped pens. Silently he chose green, and the image of the little house emerged.

What we suspected when we looked at the drawing was supported by Kim's history, behavior, and psychological testing. He was a bright child, but seriously emotionally impaired. Intellectually he could represent the parts of the house and put them together correctly, but the floating image, the emptiness of the house, and the space all around it told us that in many ways Kim still felt like a "floating abandoned object." Fortunately, Kim's new parents knew the value of seeking help for him and for themselves to help this little boy grow emotionally.

6 Years

Around age 6, the separation of the sexes becomes more pronounced for Adam and Lisa. Children begin to act out male/female roles, and normally they imitate and gradually begin to identify with the parent of the same sex. While there may still be some merging of Mommy and Daddy in pictures drawn by the twins, the female figure has become more female, and the male figure has become more male.

More and more, Adam and Lisa are becoming aware of what those large, powerful adults who direct their lives deem to be right and wrong. The twins will try to avoid or control behaviors that result in the wrath of these adult "godlike" persons. The impulses, feelings, and thoughts that inspired these now unacceptable acts have not gone. Although children are not always aware of these feelings consciously, they still can feel the need to express them. And feelings do get expressed in fantasy, in play, and in drawings—all acceptable outlets for children's emotions.

For Adam and Lisa, adjusting to first grade is a new, exciting, and demanding experience. Preschool and/or Kindergarten helped in the transition from home to school, but now they must spend at least six hours away from home—twice the time they were away last year. However, Adam and Lisa are developing their intellects and sharpening their learning skills. They are beginning to read and write short, complete sentences. This provides them with additional ways to express their emotions. The twins are learning to solve problems by dealing with Mommy and Daddy together and individually and by learning to relate to a new teacher for a longer period of the day. They need these skills to adapt to that new environment in their young lives called "school."

Adam and Lisa, and their real-life counterparts, draw objects more realistically, begin to use color more appropriately, and tell pictorial stories in greater detail.

Brent, at 6, was much more aware of the differences between boys and girls than Scott was at 5, and this is to be expected. These two drawings (for Scott's see **Fig. 65;** for Brent's see **Fig. 72**) illustrate how, within a year, normal development progresses so that drawings express greater details, more recognizable images, and compliance with parental rules.

Brent's immediate world has consisted of four people (not three) for some time, and he shows us that he has accepted that fact. This is consistent with his good adjustment to school. Although Brent has not put a ground line in his family picture, the feet of all figures are planted firmly on the bottom of the page.

Brent is the older brother of Keith, whose drawings at 4 and 5 were shown previously **(Figs. 48, 49)**. Unlike Lilly at age 4 **(Fig. 50)**, Brent acknowledges his brother's presence in the family and includes Keith in the picture, along with Mommy, Daddy and himself.

From the time he was very young, Brent was interested in using any materials he could find to express and display his creativity. His "family" portrait was produced with colored pencils and pieces of tapestry he found in his mother's sewing basket. He cut out a skirt for Mommy and pants for Daddy, Keith, and himself **(Fig. 72)**.

In the drawing, Brent is almost as tall as his father. Mommy and Daddy are distinctly different: Daddy wears a hat, and Mommy has hair. Brent still uses parts of both parents to represent himself. He has a hat like Daddy's, a nose like Mommy's, and has drawn the upper torso of himself and Mommy in the same way—with the familiar scribble.

Brent has not allowed Keith to be as big as his parents or himself, but he has given his little brother some recognition. By age 6, Brent has learned that it would not be favorable to exclude 3-year-old Keith or draw him

Figure 72

separately from the rest of the family. Brent has put a tall hat on Keith so this littlest member of the family can be equal in height, and even grants him Daddy's belly button. However, he does put himself between Keith and Mommy, taking the same position as Daddy—next to Mommy!

Looking closely at the drawing, we see that Brent has given Daddy enormous hands and each successive family member smaller and smaller hands. We do not know whether this means that Brent views Daddy as the most powerful family member or whether the large hands on Daddy, as well as the hats on heads indicate that Brent is still striving for balance. It may mean both. We know that a certain object (such as a hat or body part) may symbolize more than one thing for the person who draws that object.

Whatever the meaning (and even Brent may not be consciously aware of that meaning), there is a wonderful aspect to this artistic creation. Brent's feelings and thoughts related to his family are being expressed in a way that tells us this 6-year-old boy is learning rapidly and knows what is expected of him. He is organizing his family relationships in an orderly fashion that is comfortable to him and acceptable to everyone else.

One weekend Scott's family went fishing. When they returned, Scott at 6, drew how he felt about the adventure.

Scott did not catch a fish and neither did his mother or little sister—only his father was successful. But Scott had developed a good way to compensate for disappointment. He went to his art materials and drew what he wished would have happened. He could not quite bring himself to draw a boy catching a fish—that might have been too close to telling how he really felt. Instead, he drew a series of pictures of a girl catching a fish.

Figure 73

Figure 74

Scott's story begins with a picture of a sunset, water, and a fish; he titled it "Jumping Fish" (**Fig. 73**). The colors are appropriate. The sun is setting on the horizon line where water meets sky, and the fish really appear to be "jumping." The next drawing, titled "Fishing Girl," shows a big head with eyes, nose, smiling mouth, and lots of hair (**Fig. 74**). The figure stands on the bank and throws a line to a fish in the water. A bright yellow sun is in the upper right corner. The third drawing has the same figure, this time without hair, standing on the bank and holding the line with the fish dangling from it (**Fig. 75**). On this Scott wrote, "She Caught a Fish." In the final drawing (**Fig. 76**) the figure is smiling, holding the fish on a chain. The line and hook are drawn above the bank, and the figure appears to be falling down the bank's slope. Scott titled this one, "She Has It on Her Chane."

When we look back at Scott's ability to draw objects and people at age 5, we might think that his graphic skills have regressed in the past year. This is not true, however; he has actually improved those skills. In fact, Scott is now able to draw water and sky meeting at the horizon line, a readily recognizable fishing line, a chain, fish, and a river bank. He is even able to write complete sentences with only a few words misspelled.

Figure 75

Figure 76

What did happen between the ages of 5 and 6 was that Scott learned to overcome his disappointment by fantasizing that another child had caught the fish. It is not surprising that the other child was called a girl, as his baby sister had been on the trip, and like Brent, Scott was adjusting to including her in his immediate world. In this four-part picture story, Scott expressed his wish that he had caught a fish and did not even pretend to himself that he had been the lucky fisherman. He mastered his disappointment by drawing a girl, who by the fourth picture could easily pass for a boy—like himself and his father.

The achievements here are many: He fulfilled his fantasy vicariously; he acknowledged that there was another female in the family; and he identified with his father who had caught a fish.

Figure 77

Jon, just 6, is learning about castles and kings and queens. He uses these objects to master the constant triangle in a small child's life: two caregiving adults and self. Jon's drawing is a castle complete with turrets on the top, a wall extending from each side, three archways, and two sets of three windows (**Fig. 77**). There is one figure in each of the three archways; two figures are equal in size and larger than the third. On the heads of the two larger figures there are objects resembling crowns, while the smaller figure appears to be wearing a hat.

We have said before that it is not unusual for children around this age to show different levels of development in intellectual and emotional growth within the same drawing. Jon's portrayal of the castle is done well for a child of 6. His ability to draw figures has developed a little more slowly. Solving the problem of more grown-up relationships with Mommy and Daddy is a major task for a child, and Jon is traveling at his own slower pace.

Dayna, 6, did not accept all her siblings as readily as did Scott and Brent. We have already met Becca, Dayna's next older sister (**Fig. 68**), and we will meet Elysa, the oldest sister, in Chapter 6. We know that Dayna's brother was born when Dayna was 2 years old.

SOMETHING THAT WILL MAKE ME HAPPY

Figure 78

Using a pen with remarkable skill for a 6-year-old, Dayna has drawn a balloon with a gondola. In the gondola are five, not six, people (**Fig. 78**). We assume that one sibling is missing because there are three small and two large figures. The figures are so tiny that it is hard to tell male from female, but the largest person is smiling, standing in a row with three small figures and another larger one. We compare this with Dayna's imagery at 4 (**Fig. 11**).

The title on Dayna's picture at 6 is "Something that will make me happy." She tells us that a wonderful fantasy for her is to ride in a balloon with just the people she wants with her. She also demonstrates that she can write almost complete sentences. Like Lilly, whom you have met, Dayna handles the arrival of her brother by simply omitting him.

Cleo tells us that she, too, has learned a number of new skills in the past year. At 5, she drew one large figure with female characteristics just beginning to appear. In that drawing she also reflected her feeling of imbalance through the natural distortion of some of the limbs and body parts. At 6, Cleo creates an idyllic scene of a "couple" out walking their pets (**Fig. 79**). Her images of the woman and man are well proportioned and illustrate some skillful handling of the medium—the woman has a shoulder bag and the man has a bag in his hand. Cleo tried to show the pet leashes around the wrists of the couple, and she has drawn a house in the distance. Her artistic efforts tell us that she is observing what people do and details in her surroundings. She is aware of trees, birds, butterflies, sky, and ground. As she tries to represent them realistically, Cleo learns more about them. In this process she naturally develops new learning skills.

We know very little about Cleo, but her "couple" drawing leads us to believe that she is romanticizing what it would be like to be walking with her own male partner. Like all girls of this age, Cleo may be learning that to be like Mommy means she must also imagine her own male partner. The one she would really like to have belongs to Mommy.

Figure 79

Figure 80

Figure 81

Halloween is a time that inspires the creation of wonderful images, which are shown in the following examples from children at different ages.

In preparation for Halloween, Shelley, age 6, has drawn four people dressed for the occasion (**Fig. 80**). They are all carrying bags and I imagine they are on their way to visit homes for "trick or treat." The figures are all complete. Males are differentiated from females and the colors could be very appropriate for costumes. The four figures could very easily represent a family. Because family members are the most familiar people to a 6-year-old child, it is very possible that Shelley has used her own family members as "models."

Shelley's ability to draw figures, and organize shapes and forms to tell a story, indicates that she has very advanced learning skills. Her illustration of figures touching each other in a natural way makes us believe that touching and holding in a healthy way are usual occurrences in her home environment.

At 5, Tom drew a picture containing both female and male figures; we described how the female figure was the larger of the two. At 6, however, Tom tells us that he wants to stand alone by placing only a male figure in his drawing (**Fig. 81**). The boy Tom has created looks like he is flexing his muscles and taking a very assertive position. I suspect that the decision to draw just the image of the boy evolved as Tom was working. He did not center the figure, and, had he wanted to include another person, there is space on the paper. Tom is beginning to identify with the important male figure in his life and is trying to be less dependent on the important female in his life. His "strong" boy is not grounded by either a line or the bottom of the paper, but Tom is moving slowly in this new role. When he feels more secure, he will probably plant his feet firmly on a baseline.

Figure 82

Figure 83

Keith, at 6, is still trying to master paints. We have already described his success in creating a tree with this difficult medium at age 5. Keith now produces two figures and a building that looks like a castle resting on a green ground (**Fig. 82**). He is progressing well and does not hesitate to experiment. His pride in this image is evident—he wrote his name in bold brush strokes across the top of the page.

Warning Signals at 6

In a later chapter we will discuss at length Bobby whom we introduced to you in Chapter 1 (**Fig. 15**) and at age 4 (**Fig. 29**). We are very familiar with Bobby, and his many graphic representations of how he has been coping with the numerous surgeries on his cleft pallet. This drawing is another creative expression of how this child dealt with his problem. The "gaping mouth" that was repeated over and over in those early drawings is not present here. Instead, the jagged lines of the teeth appear on different parts of the bodies and in lines on the paper. At this age, Bobby probably is feeling much better about himself, but he may still be expressing some suppressed anger through his imagery (**Fig. 83**). This drawing is discussed in this section on "warning signals" only to illustrate how viewing one isolated drawing, without other background information, could lead us to form inaccurate conclusions.

Figure 84

Figure 85

Arthur's and Rafe's graphic representations will be discussed at length in a later chapter to illustrate how one art therapist worked with learning-disabled children in a special school setting. I refer to them here because they are very good examples of images drawn by a 6-year-old child and a 7-year-old child of average or better intelligence who were hampered by a perceptual problem (**Figs. 84, 85**). We have observed that children with this difficulty will "perseverate"—they will repeat the same answer to different questions, or become "stuck" on a word or idea, unable to move on to the next task. In drawings we see this in a repeated form or line. Most often it is a line, and in Arthur's picture he has drawn a series of lines as in **Fig. 84,** where the lines make a trail of smoke. Rafe's image show us that he has made a great deal of progress in organizing his thoughts. However, the series of lines still is present around the circle that forms an apparent tree top as well as the lines that radiate around the sun in **Fig. 85.**

We have traveled with Adam and Lisa and their real-life counterparts as they made their way from home to school, formed a normal attachment to Mommy and spread that attachment to include Daddy. Gradually they established some independence and greater awareness of self. By now this sense of self will begin to be expressed in the way they conduct themselves, particularly around each other and their parents. Adam and Lisa know they are different from each other. They have known this for several years. Lisa knows she will "grow up" to be like Mother, and Adam knows he will "grow up" to be like Father. There is still much they do not know about male/female differences, but they will ask for more information when they are ready. They are learning that the bathroom is a "private" place for one person at a time and that bedrooms have definite ownership. This natural need to identify their own "space" should be encouraged and respected as much as possible.

The next four years are a time for Adam and Lisa to acquire the knowledge and everyday living skills they will need to face adolescence.

Chapter 6

Fact-Fantasy Stage/Sequence

Around 7 To 11 years

7 Years

Adam and Lisa, just arriving home from school, race each other to the refrigerator for a snack. Mother tells them that there are cookies on the table and juice in the refrigerator—and to be quiet because their baby brother is napping. The twins collect their afternoon treat and on the way out of the kitchen Mother hears Adam announce that he is going outside to play street hockey with some of the guys; Lisa announces she is on her way upstairs to check on her Cabbage Patch doll family and is expecting her girlfriend, Anne, to come over soon to see her doll collection.

Around age 7, Adam and Lisa are very likely to go their own ways whenever possible. Both children have identified with the parent of the same sex, and for the next year or so Adam will prefer to play with boys, and Lisa will prefer the company of girls. Some parental values become so much a part of their personality that now they often act and sound like their parents on issues of "right" and "wrong." They are also acquiring new role models—teachers, television and movie stars, and sports heroes.

School continues to introduce Adam and Lisa to a variety of new learning experiences. At their own pace they will learn, through reasoning, how to move from the beginning to the end of a process and back again. Thought processes, in general, are gradually becoming more logical. They know the difference between closed forms—for example, how circles differ from squares—and they can distinguish between curved and straight lines.

The social need to communicate with peers and adults outside the home speeds the development of language skills. The use of words becomes more meaningful. Words are now an important aspect in determining the kinds of new relationships they will form and how Adam and Lisa will handle encounters with other children and adults. Like most children this age, the twins still talk to themselves, usually when struggling to solve some problem.

By now, Adam and Lisa are not likely to draw any figure that cannot be recognized as male or female. More and more, their drawings will include a ground line and horizon line. The consistent appearance of these lines tells us that Adam and Lisa are at the proper stage of development for their age, with their two feet settled firmly on the ground as they learn more about their expanding environment.

At age 7, figures may still be facing front and not showing much movement, but this will gradually change as the twins' world stretches from home to school and they engage in more active play with their new friends.

A child may use a certain color for drawing because it is the only one available or because it is the one that appeals most to the young artist's curiosity and interest in experimenting. Only when important adults press for more realistic images do Adam and Lisa begin to suppress some of their natural spontaneity and creativity. Ideally, Adam and Lisa will be given art materials with no adult rules attached. Left to express themselves freely, they will first draw what they know and then what they see. As their cognitive and artistic skills improve, children's art expressions will tell us what they know and see and feel.

Let us look at some drawings from real-life 7-year-old children.

Eva, 7, tells us much about herself in just two drawings. In the first picture (**Fig. 86**), she has drawn a figure sitting on a horse. The way the horse's legs are drawn gives the impression of movement. Rider and horse are facing what looks like a gate or fence; in horseback riding terms this could represent a hurdle. The felt-tipped markers have been used so heavily that it is not easy to see exactly where ground meets sky, but the horizon line is there. It is also difficult to tell whether the figure is male or female. The proportions of the objects—excluding the oversized sun marked with Eva's real name—are relatively the right sizes. Eva, on her horse, could jump over the hurdle.

Figure 86

In the second drawing, Eva has let everything spill out (**Fig. 87**). Obviously, she is familiar with the mythical story: Eva has titled this picture "Pandora and the Box." Pandora, with long black hair and a fancy dress, occupies the center of the picture. Around her are symbols of some of the concerns now felt by this 7-year-old child: good and bad, blindness, "cold feeling," germ, death, and poison. Some of these "worries" may seem a little unusual for such a young child, but I believe that television makes even young children aware of these possibilities. Eva also may have heard of some of these "conditions" from her parents—her mother is a special education teacher and her father is a physician. She has also included spiders, fighting, and a good spirit—objects and ideas we would expect her to know.

We do not know what Eva was thinking when she drew these pictures. They were given to us by her mother, who felt that Eva's intensity when drawing the pictures, and then putting them aside, meant that they may have had more meaning for Eva than some of the other art work she produced. This probably is true. What more marvelous symbol than something like a "hurdle" to tell us what it is like to be in school, away from home most of the day, and required to make new relationships with important adults and peers?

Eva is still sometimes uncertain whether she should *act* like a girl or a boy. But she does know that she is a girl and Pandora (a fantasized representation of herself) looms large and queenly over all the problems that may be connected to the "hurdle" in the first picture.

Brent, whom you met at age 6 (**Fig. 72**), was 7 years, 5 months old when he created a fantasy world on paper. Brent has discovered science fiction, a typical interest of boys this age in our outer space-preoccupied society. Instead of blasting off into space, however, Brent has gone under the water. Drawing on a sheet of lined notebook paper—Brent will draw on anything that has a usable surface—he created an underwater world complete with an Earth transporter and an Earth police station. Like Eva, Brent gives himself a fantasy world, but with built-in controls: the Earth police station has an open door to the "real" world through his Earth transporter (**Fig. 88**).

Figure 87

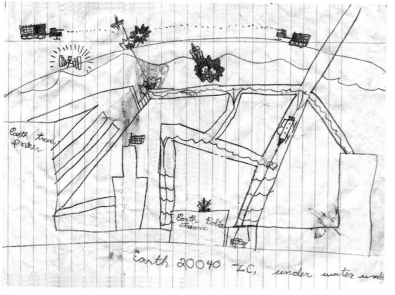

Figure 88

Children, like adults, also want to escape the "real" world when problems occur. Children will tell us in their drawings about the natural turmoil they feel around home and school. This movement is expressed in the images of magical, mythical, and scientific fantasies. For the healthy child, there will always be a growing connection to the "real" world.

Becca, 7, was beginning to make plans about what she would be when she "grew up." Naturally, these plans will change many times before she makes her final choice. Becca did two drawings within a few days of each other; together they tell a story about who she is and what she fantasizes she will be.

In the first picture Becca has drawn a smiling girl (herself), holding up one hand as if she were waving **(Fig. 89)**. On a piece of paper that she attached to the drawing, Becca wrote, "When I grow up I will be a doctor." She already knew that it was acceptable for women to consider what once was traditionally a male profession. The girl in the picture is wearing a dress; a stethoscope is hanging from her neck. Less than two weeks later, Becca has drawn a "big" girl holding the hand of a "small" boy. There is something hanging down the front of her dress in this picture, too. Although Becca did not say so, the hanging object resembles the stethoscope in the earlier drawing. The small boy may represent Becca's younger brother **(Fig. 90)**.

At this stage Becca has mixed feelings. This is a time to be like Mother and, at the same time, to be independent of Mother. Becca's drawings reflect her ambivalence about letting go and growing up. She is trying to master how she will fulfill both of these needs. She will be a "lady doctor"—not like Mother—and a lady who takes care of little children—like Mother.

Becca is one year older than her sister Dayna, who was introduced at age 6. Although she too is now 7, Dayna is not ready to plan for the future. She still wants to play outside with the dog and has drawn her wishes in a colorful image of a little girl and a rather large dog **(Fig. 91)**. Not yet comfortable with thinking as far ahead as Becca did, Dayna nevertheless makes concessions to growing up and being female. She puts rouge on her cheeks and elaborate eyelashes on her eyes. As we have mentioned before, the oversized head is seen often in the drawings of children this age. In addition to aiding in the effort to achieve balance, this overemphasis on the head also may indicate a need to pay more attention to the new experience at school.

We have shared with you the images of Keith's adjustment in preschool when he was 4; his graphic response to the concept of the creation of the world when he was 5; and his increasing ability to handle media in his painting of a tree when he was 6. At

Figure 89

Figure 90

7, Keith combined paint, pencil, and crayon to create a cartoon-like image of a snowman (**Fig. 92**). At the same time, he did a crayon drawing of a smiling boy with very broad shoulders who is tossing a football (**Fig. 93**).

We have said before that graphic images always reflect some part of the artist who has created the particular images. In addition, images speak to that moment in time. In these two pieces of artwork, Keith is telling us different feelings about himself. In the picture of the snowman, he is saying that sometimes he feels like a huge blob and a stupid fellow. We know this because Keith has the snowman saying, "Boy! I'm a stupid feller." It is also interesting that Keith had drawn three small houses. There is a tree between the two on the left, and the third house sits alone near the edge of the right side of the paper. At the time he drew this, Keith's family consisted of his older brother, father and mother. We also have learned that very often people draw the same number of objects in a picture as the number of people in their immediate family. We think that in this picture the houses represent the three males in Keith's family (including himself), and the tree represents his mother. This combination of objects and symbolic representations is not unusual for a child this age. Keith, like many 7-year-old children, is still working through his relationship with his mother and father. We also think that Keith's "stupid feller" snowman probably reflects his normal feelings of being

inferior to his older brother, partly because he was the "baby," and because he was also aware that he was small for his age.

In his next drawing (**Fig. 93**), Keith strongly compensates for any feelings of inadequacy by making himself a football player and writing his name in large letters on the picture (he did not sign the drawing of the snowman). Keith's father played fullback for his

Figure 91

Figure 92

Figure 93

college football team, and Keith's brother, Brent, plays Little League football.

We will see more of Keith's and Brent's drawings as they move toward adolescence.

The next seven drawings and paintings to be discussed come from a teacher in a public school, and aside from the children's names and ages, we know nothing about the children or their families. They are all in second grade and adjusting well to school, according to their teachers. We are very pleased to include these art expressions, because they are all different and wonderful examples of what individual children tell us when they are 7.

Shirley wants us to know that she knows what looks "male" and what looks "female." She has drawn all of the body parts for each figure and used color in a creative yet realistic way (**Fig. 94**). Shirley knows that sky is different from ground, but is still not aware that in a drawing the sky and ground meet at the horizon line.

Deana has drawn three whimsical figures riding what looks like a dinosaur (**Fig. 95**). The three important people in her life (parents and self) are

Figure 94

Figure 95

transformed into a fantasy. One of the figures carries a smaller figure; we do not know whether this represents a sibling, but it may. Deana's colors are not completely realistic, but that only helps to tell us that she is a creative and imaginative child.

Putting herself on paper as a "big" person can help a child feel like one. Rae has used almost the entire space of the paper to create this image of a woman in a hat and high-heeled shoes (**Fig. 96**). Rae apparently has learned about horizon lines; the blue sky meets the green ground.

George almost ran out of paper trying to create his "big" man—there is not enough room on the paper for the arms (**Fig. 97**). George has handled the paint very well, and artistically has painted the man in a light color against a dark background.

Figure 96

Figure 97

Dick has learned to draw objects like wheels on bicycles, and to make fancy numbers. In his drawing he is still using the familiar scribble and shapes within shapes to create a sky, but soon he will reach the developmental level of his peers and learn how to draw sky, ground and a horizon line (**Fig. 98**). He does know how to represent himself. He has drawn a smiling boy with hands on hips, standing beside a very original creation of a bike.

Figure 98

Elly's beautiful painting illustrates her continued interest in important objects in her environment—house, tree, and sun (**Fig. 99**). She also includes a bicycle, flowers, and a winding path leading to the house. The colors are realistic: a tree is green and brown, a house could be yellow and red, and a bicycle could be red. Often the way children draw windows and doors on houses makes them resemble faces. The sizes of the objects in this picture are not quite in proportion to each other. The organization of the picture, especially the way Elly has placed the house sitting on the horizon line, indicates that, if asked, she could produce all that is absent in her image without any difficulty. But why ask her to do that? Elly has taken "artistic license" and has painted how she feels in and about her surroundings. Her painting reflects her sense of balance and security in this colorful place.

Figure 99

Betty, like Keith and Elly, is still mastering that special group of three. In her own individual style of expression she has created three ballet dancers. The shorter hair on the figure in the middle makes us think this may be a male figure, but only Betty could tell us that. Her dancers are on their toes on a red stage, and they look as though they are moving (**Fig. 100**). Betty probably likes the color blue and has painted blue mouths to match the blue eyes of her dancers. As the architect of this image, Betty's use of color and its application is her expression of creativity. Betty's smiling, moving figures, in ballet costumes and toe shoes, tell us that this little girl, at 7, is learning about new people and new activities and is having fun. Her picture made us smile, too.

Figure 100

Figure 101

Warning Signals at 7

We have stated before that when we describe warning signals at any age, we are putting up a red flag and asking someone to pay close attention to this child, gather more information, and seek help if necessary. As we explore further, these warning signals may also tell us to wait—like the yellow light in a traffic signal. We must stop, look, and wait, before we move forward. In these situations we must move cautiously before we take steps toward intervention and treatment.

In Chapter 6, we described Bobby's "gaping mouth" drawing as an image that, if studied without knowing more about Bobby, would cause concern. Because it is as important to know when not to do something as it is to know when to do something, let us discuss two more examples of Bobby's drawings at age 7.

At 7, Bobby has created a Father's Day card for his "Douddy." At first glance this picture might appear to have been produced by a younger child (**Fig. 101**). However, the way in which Bobby uses different seals to design the card, and his lettering, tell us that Bobby's ability to organize his interests and thinking is normal for his age.

Bobby's second picture, obviously drawn for the same occasion, includes a picture of himself and "Daddy" (**Fig. 102**). Bobby is still drawing figures floating in space. He is still mastering shapes within shapes, just as he is mastering his trauma from repeated surgery for his cleft palate. But his figures are much more complete, telling us that he has made tremendous developmental progress in his self-image and artistic skills over the past year. Bobby is catching up with his peers, and there is no cause for concern.

There is considerable cause for concern, however, when we look at the picture of a house drawn by Rafe at age 7 (**Fig. 103**). You saw one of Rafe's drawings in Chapter 1 (**Fig. 13**). In this new picture, he has drawn a house floating in space. The image tells us he cannot make straight lines—he must draw over some of the lines to make them meet. He does know what elements make up a house; like Kim (**Fig. 1**) Rafe has drawn windows and a door. He has even included a chimney. But the struggle he portrays in trying to draw a house is a warning signal of a problem that requires further investigation. Rafe, as we discussed earlier, is a child of average intelligence who has a learning disability. This drawing alone would be a warning signal—a signal reinforced by his other drawings.

Figure 102

Figure 103

8 to 9 Years

Adam and Lisa, now age 8, continue to go their separate ways. Adam prefers to spend his time with peers of the same sex. At school he will seek the company of other boys during lunch and free periods; after school he will also spend his time in outdoor activities or indoor games with these same boys whenever possible. Competition in school achievement and in sports becomes evident, and Adam chooses friends whose accomplishments in these areas are similar to his. Adam and his friends sometimes talk about the girls in their classes and may even tease them occasionally. Usually at this age, however, they keep their distance.

Lisa's friends are girls she has met in school or in her neighborhood. Like Adam, she much prefers to be with peers of the same sex during and after school. She frequently invites girls over after school to do homework or play with dolls. Lisa and her friends also compete with each other, but this competition is more likely to be associated with scholastic achievement than with sports. However, Lisa and her friends have more opportunities for participation in sports than girls have had in the past. She will most likely become friends with girls who have similar interests; this is normal. The girls are beginning to notice the boys, whisper and giggle about them, and decide together who is "cute" and who is a "geek." They too keep their distance from their opposite sex peers.

This year and the next two are interesting years for the twins. As they learn new things in school, meet new classmates and teachers, and become acquainted with the parents of their friends, they realize that not every child or every adult is the same. It is surprising to them that a "friend" whom they thought liked the same things they did has suddenly moved on to other interests and other peer groups, and sometimes they feel left out. It is also surprising to them that some parents are more "strict" or less "strict" than their own. The twins begin to think sometimes that they have the greatest parents, while at other times they are certain their parents are the worst. This usually happens when there is a conflict about being allowed to go somewhere or acquire some new toy or piece of clothing. It is not unusual during this year and the next for the twins to fantasize that they are adopted and even dare to ask their parents for "proof" of their birth.

Adam and Lisa become much more aware of these differences among parents or caretakers during this year and the next two years. They also begin to realize that some of their friends lag behind them in some areas and that some seem to be leaving them behind.

By ages 8 and 9, children's drawings become more and more realistic, reflecting school pressures to improve their verbal, writing, and reading skills. Some children still work on art projects at home, but for others the pressure to excel academically closes the door to appreciation of the arts and free expression. Children who continue to express themselves through art will express more movement and fantasy, at the same time showing more realistic proportions in the relationships between objects in a drawing.

We now describe some drawings from real-life 8- to 9-year-old children. Elysa has drawn a "self-portrait" at 8 1/2 years. She presents a profile of a little girl standing in the grass, looking very content, with a big smile on her face (**Fig. 104**). This picture also communicates that Elysa at 8 1/2 is still drawing a figure with a large head and has not yet learned how to represent the horizon line. But her skill in drawing a profile and in attention to detail also tell us that she is expanding her artistic skills at her own pace.

We said previously that Halloween is a time that always inspires young artists to create fantastic images. Brent, 8 years, 7 months, struggled to put all of his images on one piece of paper and discovered that he was running out of space (**Fig. 105**). A sitter was with him when Brent was working on this picture, and he expressed his frustration to her. She suggested that he tape another piece of paper to the bottom of the first. Brent was delighted with this solution—he now knew how to solve the problem of running out of space on paper. He now also had enough room to include all of the objects that for him represented Halloween—a haunted house, flying witches and bats, pumpkin faces, and a black cat hunched on a fence. We met Brent's family earlier in a picture he created at 6 (**Fig. 72**) and learned about his fantasy of an underwater world at 7 (**Fig. 88**).

Figure 105

Figure 104

A friend had a wonderful way of teaching the children in her classroom new words to add to their vocabulary. She would give the children a large sheet of paper, instructing them to write eight new words on this sheet and illustrate each word. She would also have them move to the words and make a sound they thought would be connected to each word.

Ron, 8, did this series of images to show his understanding of "run," "shoot," "kick," "jump," "fight," "work," "cry" and "bark" (**Fig. 106**). Looking at his individual representations, we can see that Ron understands the words and has learned how to draw movement and action, creating his own symbols for different words and ideas.

Nina, another child in the same school class, was given the names of states and countries—"Texas," "Mississippi," "Washington," "New York," "Mexico," "California," "Iran" and "Hawaii"—and asked to draw them. At 8, Nina is learning a great deal about different places and has selected objects meaningful to her to represent each place symbolically. For example, she has drawn a river for Mississippi, a tall monument for Washington and palm trees for Hawaii (**Fig. 107**). The way that Nina makes connections and solves problems presented to her tells us that she is progressing very well in school and is becoming more aware of the world around her.

Figure 106

Figure 107

Etta, 8, still focuses on three objects, and has shown us that on some level she is still preoccupied with the most important relationships in her young life—Mommy, Daddy, and self (**Fig. 108**). Etta has painted a colorful picture of three figures. From the clothing on the figures it was difficult to tell whether they are females or males; in real life both boys and girls wear pants. However, two of the figures have long hair, suggesting that the one with short hair may be a male figure. Etta is able to portray movement—the arms are all in different positions. She also makes the sky meet the ground at a horizon line, and can control paint to produce a complex image.

Figure 108

Sonny, 8, is experimenting with different media and discovering how to create intricate designs in black and white, using stems and flowers as his inspiration (**Fig. 109**). The control of the lines and the organization in this picture tell us that Sonny has noticed his surroundings and can organize his impressions of them.

Figure 109

Figure 110

Jamie told me she loves to draw landscapes and sent this picture to me along with a drawing of a female figure. Her drawing of trees, grass, sun, sky, clouds and flowers is organized, colorful, and recognizable. The trees are all grounded on the grass and the sky meets the ground (**Fig. 110**). The image of the girl, while not grounded, is complete, and like Elysa above, Jamie still sometimes puts a big head on her figures (**Fig. 111**). Learning new skills, like horizon lines and ground lines, doesn't mean that they will appear in every graphic production. We will see some of Jamie's early drawings in a later chapter. These drawings tell us that she is continuing to develop normally.

Figure 111

Figure 112

Lisa, like Jamie, likes to do artwork and also sent me some new draw-ings. Lisa is 9 and one of her drawings depicts a feeling of nervousness and excitement. She has drawn a girl, about her own age, complete with eye-lashes, long hair, jeans, and a flowered shirt **(Fig. 112)**. The arms and one foot are up; the other foot is firmly planted on a bed of tacks, nail up; in a cartoon blurb she has written, "boy I'm nervous." She titles her picture, "I'm on pins and needles." There is a big smile on the girl's face, so the tacks do not appear to be too painful. Lisa's drawing tells us she has learned to make images that are consistent with her age.

Warning Signals at 8 to 9

In previous chapters we met Scott, a very creative child who receives a great deal of encouragement to draw at home. At 8, Scott produced a very organized drawing by placing one color next to another to make different shapes **(Fig. 113)**. But most of his previous drawings showed a freedom with the medium and subject matter that is not present here. Even when Scott mastered his dislike of a snowman and drew him as a robot at age 7 1/2, he was more expressive and creative. Because I know Scott and have

Figure 113

been very familiar with his artistic productions since he was 3, I wondered what stimulated this very tight, structured drawing. In fact, it reminded me very much of the kinds of drawings produced by nurses and medical students when asked to draw for the first time in years (this observation will be further discussed in a later chapter). I asked Scott's mother if she had any idea of what may have prompted Scott to produce this image, so unlike any of his others.

His mother did have an answer. Scott's father had gone out of town on a business trip for a few days. Shortly after he left, Scott received a call from a friend who told him he had just learned that his father had gone away and was never returning. Immediately after reporting this telephone conversation to his mother, Scott went to his room, did this drawing, and then moved on to another activity. It was also very unlike Scott not to show his artist mother his pictures and discuss them with her. Scott's mother and I both believe that after his friend's "news," Scott probably began to worry that maybe his father would not return either. The concentration required to make these colored shapes within shapes (a preoccupation with an earlier form of expression) seemed to relieve some of the anxiety we believe Scott was feeling temporarily—an anxiety seen in the pressured way Scott used the crayons.

Learning to make designs with new media in school is expected at ages 8 to 9, as we saw in Etta's painting. However, when a child produces a spontaneous picture that is so very different from everything else he or she is creating at that time, as Scott did, it is important to notice whether this kind of expression continues and to try to learn if there is anything troubling the child. In this case the anxiety was based on a fear that, for Scott, was not a reality. Scott did not duplicate this image, and there was no need to discuss this picture with him.

Becca drew a picture of herself with a stethoscope around her neck when she was 7 (**Fig. 89**), and she wrote about her wish to be a doctor when she grew up. We predicted that she would change her mind many times before reaching a final decision. At 8, Becca drew a picture of a figure she titled, "self-portrait," and she attached a story in which she reported that she washes dishes and wants to be an artist (**Fig. 114**). We would expect Becca to want to identify with her mother (an artist), and we would also expect to see this drawing indicate normal developmental progress in the same way her earlier ones did. At 8, Becca's drawing of a figure was less mature than her drawing at 7. Like Scott, Becca seems to be telling us that something is troubling her this time. Being aware that a sudden shift in creative expression may be a warning signal will alert us to observe our children's developmental progress more closely.

We do not know what was going on with Becca at the time, but I was able to share this observation with Becca's mother so that she would be sensitive to Becca's struggle with identity issues during adolescence. The last we heard, Becca had grown up just fine; she was in college and doing very well.

Around 7 years, Elizabeth had some feelings of anxiety related to her school performance. Her concerned parents discussed this matter with her teachers, who were also concerned. A medical examination had revealed no obvious physical reason for the anxiety. Elizabeth is a beautiful, bright, talented little girl, who loves to draw. For this reason, it was recommended that she meet with me to try to determine why she was so worried. At the time of this writing,

Figure 114

Elizabeth agreed to share two of her drawings, which we both knew were very important in the understanding she was gaining.

From the beginning, I was impressed with her intelligence and artistic talent. During one of our first meetings, shortly before she was 8, I asked Elizabeth to draw her family (**Fig. 115**). In the picture she has made a very good realistic representation of her father, mother and older brother, all in proportion to each other. But Elizabeth has drawn herself like a Cabbage Patch doll rather than a real person.

Figure 115

Some months later, Elizabeth has drawn a picture of what she does when she is angry or upset—she cries (**Fig. 116**). Here, the image of herself is much more realistically portrayed as the real, pretty young girl that she is. Elizabeth, her family, and I know that these two drawings, made months apart, show us that Elizabeth is beginning to have a better image of herself and is more able to express her feelings than she had been able to in the past. She still draws members of her beloved Cabbage Patch doll family, but they are no longer self-portraits. Her images of family members also have improved.

Figure 116

Carl, 8, is in the same school class as Ron **(Fig. 117)** and Nina, but his drawing tells us that he is not doing as well as they are. Some of the illustrations for his words look like they have been drawn by a much younger child. The way he drew the faces and hats for "Mexico," and the moving arms in his figure symbol for "New Jersey," shows us he is probably of average or above-average intelligence **(Fig. 118)**. However, the fact that he has not completed figures and draws in a constricted, colorless way warns us that he may not have a very good self-image. Normal children at this age usually feel pretty good about themselves, and those good feelings about self are essential in helping Carl (and all children) find their way through the normal upheaval of adolescence. Carl may be having some emotional problems. Fortunately, his teacher is aware of this and knows where and how to obtain help if necessary.

Figure 117

Figure 118

Ken produced three drawings during the school year when he was around 8 1/2. He is a learning-disabled child who attends a special school. Ken's problem is that he is hyperactive. His drawings show us he has difficulty staying within boundaries, real or imagined. His picture of the "Battle of Gettysburgh" indicates he has worked very hard to organize the battlefield and draw the North and South sections, with the river between, but he is not able to achieve his goal (**Fig. 119**).

Ken has also tried to draw "A Tornado" and "A Tital Wave" and has been unable to control his movements on paper; this picture is more scribbled than drawn (**Fig. 120**).

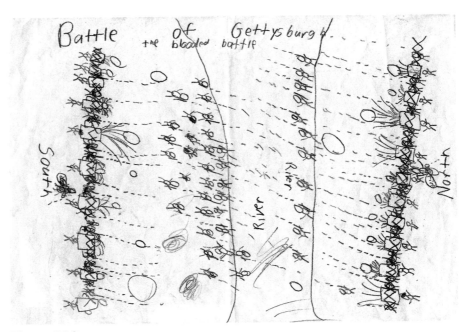

Figure 119

Figure 120

Ken has also drawn "Super Rabbit" (**Fig. 121**). While this shows a little more control, the form is clearly not consistent with images drawn by other children of his age. Here too, Ken is unable to stay within the boundaries he personally established; he is compelled to scribble in and around the figure. Ken is receiving special attention in his school setting, including medication and art therapy. It is hoped that intervention and treatment eventually will help Ken to function better and move forward developmentally.

Another 8-year-old boy, Dick, also was diagnosed as hyperactive. Because of his behavior it was assumed that he also suffered from minimal brain dysfunction and was placed in a special classroom. He was referred to a colleague of mine for movement therapy to help him control his hyperactive body movements. The movement therapist, Mrs. Dulicai, began to suspect that this child was emotionally disturbed and did not have any minimal brain dysfunction. For a number of years, Mrs. Dulicai and I have worked together, using both art and movement/dance therapy approaches with individuals, families, and groups, training students in both modalities. It is not unusual for us to share our professional concerns, and Dick's evaluation and progress reflects this collaboration.

To test Mrs. Dulicai's belief that Dick did not have minimal brain dysfunction, I decided to ask him to make two drawings of a house—directing him to draw the first very quickly, and to take as much time as he wanted needed in the second (top and bottom of **Fig. 122**). As you can see, the top drawing resembles some of the artwork made by Ken, loose and scribbled over. However, when Dick is allowed to draw at his own pace, no evidence of minimal brain dysfunction or hyperactivity appears.

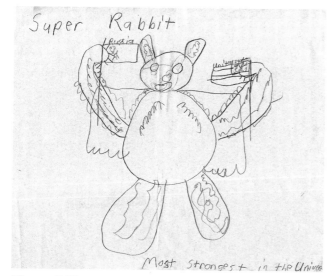

Figure 121

Figure 122

The way in which Dick drew the house and tree in unrealistic proportions offers another warning signal. At 8, this is not typical. Further investigation by Mrs. Dulicai confirmed her suspicion that Dick's emotional problems were interfering with his ability to learn. Movement therapy sessions then focused on Dick's emotional problems. Counseling sessions with his mother also were held, and within the year, he was able to return to a normal classroom setting.

9 And 10 Years

At 9, Adam still prefers the company of boys, and his interests continue to center around school activities and sports. He and his friends will get together as frequently as they can during school and after. Adam is particularly pleased when he and some of his classmates are invited into a game of baseball with some of the older boys. Weather permitting, the boys will play games—basketball, kickball, street hockey and football. Sometimes on a weekend or after dinner Adam's father or mother or one of the other boys' parents will join them. Adam does not always feel like playing in a game and some days is content just to watch.

When the weather brings the boys indoors, there is always television and a myriad of computer games. Adam and his friends have their favorite rock stars. They very likely have a radio, cassette, or CD player blaring, regardless of what else they are doing. This does not always please the adults in the house, and compromises must be negotiated between Adam and his parents about when and where in the house he can listen to his music.

Other areas of compromise begin to occur around the issues of what Adam wants to wear to school (probably the same T-shirts and cut off jeans his friends are wearing), what games and sports equipment he must have, and how much money he needs to "go places" with the boys on the weekend.

Lisa and her friends are not playing with their dolls as much as they did during the previous year, but the dolls and stuffed animals are still very much part of the decor in their bedrooms. Gymnastic activities after school are appealing, and sports are more available for girls than they were in the past. Lisa finds new friends who share her expanding interests, which include her special favorites among the rock stars. And this is a time when Lisa and her friends plan weekend sleepovers.

Clothes are also becoming an important item for Lisa. She and her friends will try to convince their parents that they must have a special sweater or a certain style shoe—whatever makes them feel like they are part of the group. Lisa loves to go shopping with mother or some of her friends on a weekend, checking out jewelry and makeup counters and imagining what they will buy when they are grown up.

In spite of these activities that are still decidedly female and male things and the impact of the feminist movement, TV, and new cultural norms, it is not unusual to see Adam or some of his friends interested in what was formerly considered just for girls and interest from Lisa and some of her friends in activities previously assigned to boys.

Sometimes it seems as if they are squeezing their school work in between all of these peer activities, but most of the time Adam and Lisa realize that school is very important. They also know that if they do not attend to their schoolwork, they will be in trouble with parents and teachers.

As the twins reach age 10 and approach age 11, they realize that more and more is expected of them. Adam and Lisa are expected to do their homework; they are expected to take care of their personal hygiene; they are expected to understand why they cannot have everything they want. Parents, caregivers, and teachers are setting new limits. Lisa and Adam are not always willing to comply and this causes some friction between them and the adults in their world. They are beginning to realize that for now, they must accept these limits. This is not always an easy time for the adults around them. As preadolescents, Adam and Lisa will communicate in subtle and not so subtle ways that they are not pleased with these controls. Parents, caregivers, and teachers need to acknowledge and accept this reaction because it is normal. At the same time, they need to remember that setting limits will eventually help the twins establish their own boundaries as responsible adults.

Other important and interesting things are happening at this time. Adam, Lisa, and their friends are becoming more aware of their bodies. They notice some of the girls growing taller faster than the boys, and some girls are growing breasts earlier than others. Privately, the girls discuss menstruation and its relation to having babies. When not able to find an answer to a particular question about these subjects, Lisa will probably ask her mother, or an adult female with whom she feels comfortable, to explain. Only when Adam can't get the answers he wants from his peers, will he approach his father, an older brother, or a male relative he feels he can talk to.

Some 9- to 10-year-olds attend boy-girl parties, but they are not much fun. Generally the boys will sit in one corner and, depending on how much TV they are allowed to watch, try to act "cool." The girls will probably be in another part of the room, still in the giggling stage and trying to decide how to get the boys to dance. Regardless of how grown up they may try to act, children at this age still are not ready to socialize with peers of the opposite sex.

This is a time in children's lives when they experience preadolescent anxiety. Some of Lisa's and Adam's friends long to jump into adolescence and others are holding back. The twins notice that some friends act older and leave them behind, while others now seem too young for them.

Intellectually, the twins are developing learning skills that enable them to follow a thought process from beginning to end. They can identify new learning problems and understand new ways to solve them. They understand the concept of conservation and sequencing. For examples, they know that pouring a glass of water into different-sized bottles does not change the amount of water, and they can put objects in size order, from smallest to largest, and then reverse the process.

The art productions of 9- and 10-year-old children will show that this is a time when familiar objects are represented realistically. Baselines are elevated and ground lines are clearly drawn. Objects and people are illustrated in frontal and profile views and show action. People and objects in the environment will be in realistic proportion to each other. The subject matter will show us the facts the children are learning and their fantasies, as they move through later childhood and approach the normal upheaval of adolescence.

Figure 123

Some of Adam's and Lisa's real-life counterparts show us these facts and fantasies in their drawings.

Like some pictures we saw previously in this chapter, the first seven art productions described were created by children from the same school district and represent different ethnic and religious backgrounds. Their teacher reports they were all performing academically at age-appropriate level. We know nothing about these children except their age, sex, and what they tell us about themselves in their pictures.

Vera, 9, knows quite a bit about baseball. She has drawn a baseball player "up to bat." He is standing on the base, feet in position, arms up, ready to swing his bat (**Fig. 123**). His baseball uniform is handsomely painted in red and white. Vera also knows sky meets ground, and she is able to keep the paint from smearing so that everything she wants to say is carefully and clearly illustrated. She is also telling us she wants to play ball like the boys.

Rita, at 9 is also interested in a sports that is usually assumed to be just for boys. She has drawn two girls and a boy playing football on a field of grass (**Fig. 124**). One girl appears to be getting ready to kick, while the other girl reminds us of a cheerleader. The boy on the side is holding a football. Rita's figures are all in motion and in realistic proportion to each other. Her decision to show just three players leads us to believe that Rita may still be working through her transition from home to school and peers, which is not unusual for this age. What is important is that Rita's painting does show us that she is at the proper cognitive and social levels for her age.

Figure 124

José, 9, seems to have a real appreciation for flowers. He has creatively painted a pink flower with a yellow center, placing it on a blue background **(Fig. 125)**. The way José used all the space on the paper and applied the paint with sweeping brush strokes tells us that he has been encouraged to express himself creatively and had acquired the necessary skills to do so.

Aaron, 9, has discovered prizefighting. His drawing of two prizefighters and the referee is remarkably detailed for a child of his age **(Fig. 126)**. Aaron has drawn one fighter knocked to the canvas; the other fighter is being proclaimed the winner by the referee over a microphone. Aaron has missed no detail, and the smile on the "winner's" face tells us that this young artist feels good about himself. Aaron should feel pleased. His drawing indicates that he is functioning on an advanced intellectual level and can clearly represent anything he chooses.

Figure 125

Figure 126

Figure 127

Figure 128

Figure 129

At 9, Bert is as capable as José in depicting people and objects in his environment that interest him. Bert has illustrated a room equipped with a work table, shelves, desk, and desk chair, in which a man and woman are working (**Fig. 127**). The realistic way in which Bert has drawn one figure facing front and the other figure in profile, both holding objects, demonstrates that Bert's artistic and learning skills are better than average.

Cathy, also 9, has painted a colorful picture of three ladies, all dressed brightly and in different positions. We cannot tell whether Cathy's figures are dancing or walking, and we are not quite sure what two of the women are holding (**Fig. 128**). Cathy seems to have a little more difficulty in handling paint than some of her peers, but her organized, creative composition communicated that Cathy knows what she wants to express and is doing it well for her age.

Sheila tells a story about a girl walking along a street, pulling a small child in a wagon (**Fig. 129**). We do not know whether Sheila, who is 9, has a younger brother or sister, or is romanticizing about growing up and pulling her own child in a wagon. She has written the word "love" on the top step leading to the door of the house she has placed behind the figures. Sheila's picture, so carefully executed, conveys the importance this scene has for her and that she is capable of expressing herself creatively.

These seven children have shown us, through their artistic productions, their own unique interests. The way in which they are able to express these interests tells us that they show developmental progress normal for their age. Some are a little more advanced than others, which may mean that some are able to learn more easily than others and have had more encourage-

Figure 130

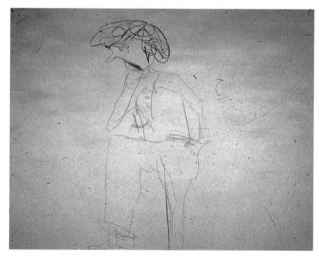

Figure 131

Figure 132

ment to be creative. As we saw, a few of these children are moving along the developmental path a little more slowly, at their own pace.

You met Elysa when she was 8 1/2. At that time we mentioned that she had not yet learned to represent a horizon line, and at 9 1/2 she was still separating sky and ground in her drawings. By age 10, Elysa has caught up and perhaps is moving ahead of her peers. For a school project she has created an intricate design in black and white. The elaborate and sophisticated way in which Elysa solves this assignment revealed that she was able to address problems on an advanced intellectual level (**Fig. 130**).

At this age, Elysa can also tell us that she is approaching adolescence with normal concerns about herself. In **Fig. 131**, she has drawn a figure in profile leaning on a raised knee. The mouth is drawn so that it almost looks like a moustache, and there is an earring on the ear. It is not unusual for a child of this age to begin to draw figures that combine female and male characteristics. Adolescence is a time when this question of identity must be faced once again. At 10, Elysa's figure drawing, in profile, suggests that she is not yet ready to "face" this task, or "move" too quickly. Although the figure is grounded on the bottom of the page, one foot is cut off by the bottom of the page.

We know from Dayna's drawing at age 4 (**Fig. 11**), and other productions, that she enjoyed artwork and generally drew images reflecting her activities and fantasies like other children her age. At 9, however, Dayna produced a crayon drawing that is at once colorful, tightly controlled, and very different from her other pictures (**Fig. 132**). This picture immediately reminded me of Scott's drawing produced when he was anxious about his father's absence (**Fig. 113**).

I could not help wondering whether Dayna's image was also expressing concern about a real or imagined loss. Some months later, I spoke to Dayna's mother, and she confirmed my assumptions. The family's beloved housekeeper, who had been with the family since Dayna was an infant, had retired around the time Dayna did this picture. Unlike Scott, Dayna felt a real loss, but like Scott, was filling in different areas and shapes with heavy crayon lines as a was to "contain" the strong feelings connected with this separation.

Keith, 9, has been drawing fantasy characters for months. You have seen Keith's art work at 4 (**Figs. 48, 49**), at 5 (**Figs. 61, 62, 63**), and at 7 (**Figs. 94, 95**). Keith knew this work was in process, and he and three of his friends wanted to be represented. They sent a book of characters they created and titled, "THE DUDES." It is so typical of preadolescents to create funny, bizarre and strange characters, to project different images as they experience physical changes, and to display some uneasiness as they approach the teen years. It also is one way they can imaginatively express thoughts and feelings about who they will be (or not be) when they grow up.

At 9, Keith has drawn a strange-looking character, with one green eye and one red eye, with a red high hat perched on the side of his head (**Fig. 133**). Keith calls his picture "Jamaican Jugee." This "person" in Keith's picture is kneeling on a green hill, high above everything with his head and most of his body in the clouds. The colors and the details have been applied with great care. We do not know what this figure means to Keith, but we learned that he spent days completing it.

Another character created by Keith, named "Jamaican Juji," was elaborately detailed in pencil (**Fig. 134**). This figure has hair standing on end, bloodshot eyes, and a mouth that appears to be screaming. "Juji" appears to be shocked by what he sees, and he is not nearly so "lofty" as is Keith's "Jamaican Jugee." What fantasies of Keith's this figure reflects are also unknown to us. But both drawings tell us that this child is able to show us intellectually and emotionally his wildest fantasies in a way that is acceptable and appropriate for his age.

Figure 133

Figure 134

Figure 135

At 9, Keith's friend and co-creator of "THE DUDES," Milton, created "BUBBA" (**Fig. 135**). With two sets of ears, squiggly hair, wrinkled brow and odd features, "BUBBA" does not look like anyone we know. The drawing does tell us that the artist who produced this is very clever and imaginative for his age.

The other co-creators of "THE DUDES" happen to be 11, and we include them here to demonstrate how different, and at the same time similar, children are betweem 9 and 11 years.

Simon, 11, chose to make a female character called "SHIRLEY." She has pigtails, wide eyes, and very little body identified by what looks like a collar on a shirt (**Fig. 136**). Simon has learned to shade objects with a pencil, giving dimension to the face he has drawn. Although the facial features are feminine, there are no female characteristics in the part of the body that is seen. This is not surprising, for Simon is closer to adolescence than Keith and Milton. Like Elysa, presented above, he is probably beginning to be aware of some of the tasks related to his physical development that he will have to "face."

Figure 136

Alan, also 11, avoids the issue of doing a male or female character. Instead, he draws a "PEANUT HEAD" with droopy eyes, odd nose and mouth with a cigar hanging out of one side **(Fig. 137)**. The caricature also has a skinny neck, but no body.

All four of these boys have cleverly allowed us a glimpse of their fanciful views of themselves and others during the week they designed "THE DUDES."

Another boy between ages 9 and 10 had an entirely different style to communicate his thoughts and feelings consistent with this age. Don drew two pictures at the request of his teacher. The first was a spontaneous drawing of a huge figure with a pumpkin head, standing over a figure that has been stabbed. Feelings of aggression and anger are normal at this age, and Don knew by now that to express them directly was not acceptable. But he also knew that by creating unreal characters he can express any of his feelings on paper **(Fig. 138)**.

Don's second picture was a family portrait. It is clear in this image that he does not view his sisters (females) in the same way he views himself, his parents, and his brothers. His sisters barely look human, while everyone else seems to have a very normal face. He omitted all human bodies, but drew a huge dog (no doubt the family pet) almost complete at the bottom of the page **(Fig. 139)**. We have said before that omission of body parts at specific ages is a warning signal. However, we know that Don can draw very realistically when he wants to, and at this preadolescent stage, it is not unusual to see incomplete figures.

Figure 137

Figure 138

Figure 139

Warning Signals at 9 to 10

Anne, 10, was in Don's class and also drew a family portrait for her teacher. At first glance, we are impressed with Anne's ability to draw very detailed and complete figures. However, the teacher's note on the picture told us that Ann had several unrealistic excuses for not including herself—"she didn't fit," "she couldn't draw herself"—and did so only on the third request. We also noticed that she put herself at a distance from the rest of the family and that everyone is floating in space. Anne has placed a sun in the upper right **(Fig. 140)**. Children this age are normally confronted with the need to gain distance from their families as they come closer to adolescence, but Anne's reluctance to include herself at all, the absence of a ground line, and the presence of the sun drawn like that of a very young child, in contrast to the very sophisticated way she drew the figures, point to inconsistencies that warrant close observation of Anne's behavior and her interactions with peers and adults.

Figure 140

Another child in the same class as Don and Anne drew a picture that raised many concerns about her intellectual and emotional development. Elaine, 9, drew a tree, rainbow, birds and cloud (**Fig. 141**). These images are typical of those produced by children around age 4 and 5 years. This is a warning signal that something may be wrong.

Mickey and Pam, both 9 years old, have also shown us cause for concern in the way they illustrated their families. Mickey drew stick figures without any hands or feet (**Fig. 142**). We have said that omissions at this age are not unusual, but the floating forms, her childlike attempt to distinguish between females and males, and the "potato head" faces all suggest that Mickey is functioning on a level much lower than his chronological age.

Pam (**Fig. 143**) has put a ground line under her family figures, but they have been drawn like those of a child aged 5 or 6. Both of these children's pictures contain serious warning signals.

It is of importance to note that these children were in the fourth grade of a public school and giving no indication of having any problems. Their school performance was reported to be average and they were not known to behave inappropriately. Very often the quiet, average child will show no overt signs of problems.

We do know something about Jason, 10 years of age. He moved from a rural community to an urban one and was sent to a special school for learning disabilities. One of his early drawings, produced for the art therapist in his school, led the staff to believe that Jason's immaturity and stress over the family's recent move caused his learning problems, not brain damage as suspected at first. In this in-

Figure 141

Figure 142

Figure 143

Figure 144

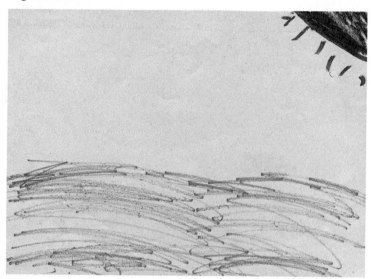
Figure 145

stance the warning signals in Jason's drawings helped to define the origin of his problems, providing data to enable his classroom teachers and art therapist to work together to help him "ground" himself in his new and frightening environment, the city.

His drawings tell us how Jason progressed over the next year. In the first, he has used his fingers, covered with charcoal, to make circles above the scribbled ground (**Fig. 144**). There is much more ground in **Fig. 145** and the sun has made a partial appearance in the upper corner. Several months later, Jason began to make images that represent realistic objects in proportion to each other, with a ground line under them (**Fig. 146**). Near the end of the school year, Jason produced this wonderful drawing in which he presented a house, a tree, a smiling little boy and a snowman, all grounded and in proportion to each other (**Fig. 147**). This picture, seen without benefit of the others and without information about this child, would surely be a warning signal. Jason still is not functioning at the level of his peers, but with support he can continue to progress and gain some of the intellectual and emotional skills needed to handle the challenges of adolescence.

Figure 146

Figure 47

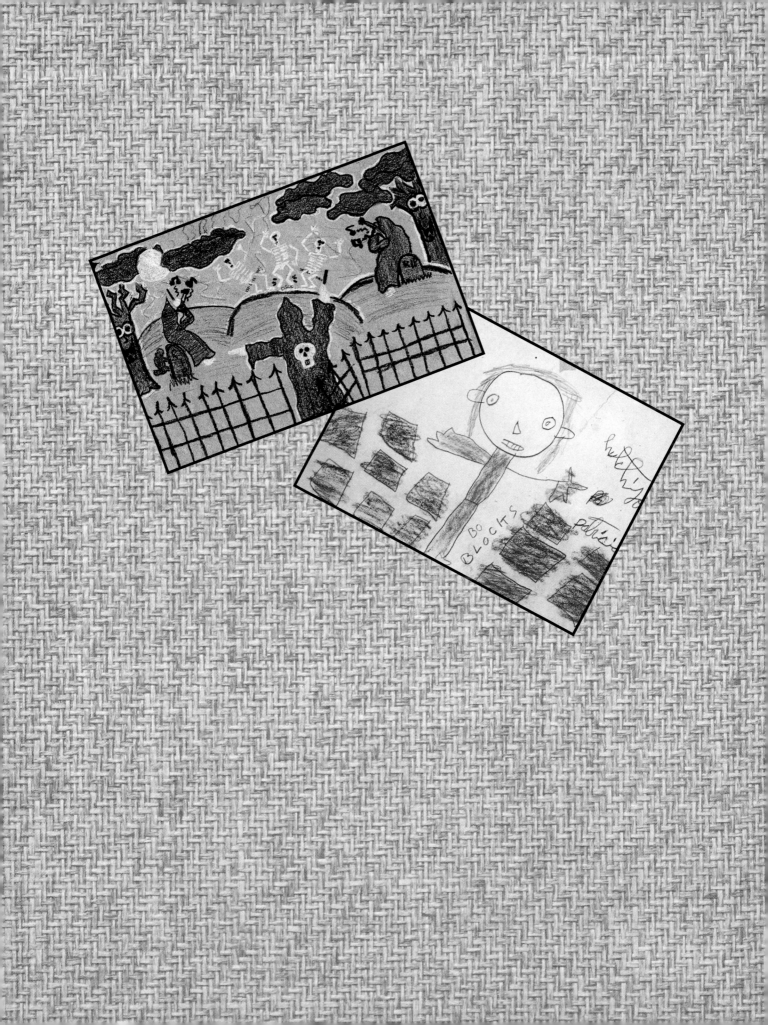

Chapter 7

The End of the Beginning

By the time children reach age 11, they are approaching the end of those developmental stages/sequences that must prepare them for the bumpy road of adolescence and eventual adulthood. Childhood is behind them. Most appropriately for this kind of book, the critical first decade of a child's life can be described very well through a child's picture.

I am fairly certain that Brent, 11, was not thinking of either childhood or adolescence when he produced a Halloween picture for a school competition—he was thinking of winning the competition and having his drawing hung in the hallway of his school (**Fig. 148**). Brent has drawn a ghost orchestra. The conductor, with his back to the viewer, stands inside an open gate facing the musicians who are sitting on tombstones and playing their instruments. Skeletons dance in the background, and tree stumps

Figure 148

have smiling faces. Brent has woven his name above the clouds. We do not know whether the ghosts represent the past or the future, but Brent has drawn himself on a threshold, not looking behind but facing the unknown. On the back of the picture Brent explained that his inspiration for this was a musical composition, "Dance Macabre" by Saint-Saens.

You have met Brent many times before and know that he has now acquired many of the skills needed to orchestrate his way through his gate and his dance.

We think of another child who was not so fortunate as Brent and many of the other normal children presented in these pages. Pat was a 17-year-old "child" when I met her in a state hospital many years ago. She had been diagnosed as schizophrenic, and the staff considered her a problem patient because she was uncooperative. She did like to draw flowers and figures and to fill in squares. One of my students brought Pat's drawings to my attention because they did not seem to be typical of those produced by other schizophrenic patients. They were not. They were, in fact, like those frequently produced by mentally retarded adults. An example of Pat's work is a drawing of a little girl with outstretched arms, standing in the middle of a number of blocks (**Fig. 149**). Pat cannot write her name correctly, nor can she stay within the lines of her blocks. Psychological testing confirmed that Pat was brain damaged and that her "uncooperativeness" was a manifestation of both her inability to learn and her frustration. At 17, Pat did not have the skills to "orchestrate" her future.

These examples help to remind us about the point of this book. Seeing what your children are telling you in their creative expressions will help you lead them in their early years, so they can learn how to lead themselves.

We have stated several times that adolescence is a turbulent period and have also said that this phase of development would require another book. Fortunately, most of us have forgotten the difficult times we experienced between 11 and 17 years. A brief explanation of why these years are naturally so difficult may help you, parents, teachers, and caregivers, to appreciate fully the importance of mastering developmental tasks in the earlier years.

Figure 149

Normal physical development of male and female characteristics makes girls and boys aware of their bodies and those of their peers. They also realize that they can now fulfill sexual fantasies and that they must reestablish values that were taken for granted when they were younger. It is a time for children to test limits, to find new role models to help them become independent, to define their own identity, and to separate from their parents. We call this the "second" separation-individuation period, the "first" having occurred around the age of 2 1/2 to 3 years. This separation-individuation is a major task that must be confronted and mastered so that adulthood can be achieved. Adolescence is normally chaotic, but without the mastery of the first ten years, the adolescent cannot make order out of this chaos.

Every intellectual advance of children must be mastered before they can move to the next level. This is not necessarily true of emotional development. Children are able to move from the infant stage to the toddler stage, and so on, without having mastered the previous stage emotionally. We have said that artistic skills parallel learning skills, and if the child is progressing normally, these advances will be evident in their creative expressions. If these normal advances are impeded for any reason, children's drawings will tell us that something is wrong. So long as a child is physically able to handle an art medium and is encouraged to use it, drawing and painting will be done naturally, regardless of whether these skills are developmentally appropriate.

Picture an army of soldiers traveling through a war zone. They win some battles and they lose some—and some of the soldiers never get through. Now think of an infant born with normal biological and emotional attributes needed to master the developmental tasks of each stage/sequence of development. If problems encountered along the way are not resolved, these attributes will be unable to mature and strengthen. Let us look, for example, at the stage/sequence of 18 months to 3 years of age. During this time the toddler is struggling with learning to control bodily functions. If those responsible for guiding the child through this difficult period are themselves ambivalent and/or inconsistent in their approach to the child, some of the normal biological and emotional attributes will be impaired—like wounded soldiers, unable to move on to the next battle. Each new stage/sequence is an arena in which the normally growing child must confront and master new tasks before moving on to the next.

Let us review what children tell us in their art.

Understanding children's drawings is one method for assessing developmental progress. Drawings can be a powerful and efficient source of clues to the intellectual and emotional life of children that may not be immediately apparent in behavior. In some cases artistic productions will provide information to support some observable behavior. If that behavior is abnormal, images produced in any medium can direct the art psychotherapist to search for the apparent sources of a problem. Identifying these sources may require input from several specialists before the problem can be diagnosed, and resolution of the problem may require the collaboration of other professional therapists.

Whether you are the parent, teacher, or designated care-giver, recognizing the normal indicators of intellectual and emotional growth in a child's imagery can tell you whether the child is thinking, learning, and feeling in the same way as normal children around that age. The danger signals you can recognize are a message telling you to ask for help. This next section will review briefly the indicators and danger signals noted in detail in Chapters 3 through 6.

We know that children cannot even begin to scribble until they can grasp a crayon, and this does not occur until they are at least 18 months of age. Nor can this occur if Mommy or Daddy or a significant adult does not provide crayon and paper for them. Their behavior tells us that children at this age need to be supervised, for they are still likely to put whatever they can into their mouths, or scribble on any surface available.

If a child between 18 months to 2½ years does not show any signs of interest in scribbling, or seems to be unable to pursue it, you should be warned that something may be wrong physically or mentally and have your child evaluated.

Initially, scribbles are produced for the pure joy of moving the arms. Gradually the toddler begins to delight in colors and lines and begins to combine them to make shapes within shapes. This usually happens around age 3.

The scribble continues to take form, and shapes are outlined and placed within other shapes by around 2 1/2 to 4 years of age. During this period of growth, children will begin to draw more complex images, and they will experiment with paint and clay if these materials are offered. Even though the child is now learning words and parts of sentences, children rarely have a plan in mind when they begin to create an image. However, if you ask, they may tell you what they have drawn.

Around 4, children are able to draw circles, squares, and triangles. Recognizable forms take shape, sometimes by accident and sometimes by design. They connect circles with lines to create a face, arms, and legs, or a sun with lines extending from it.

As intellectual and artistic skills improve around ages 5 and 6, children's drawings will tell us about the objects they know and see in their environment. Naturally, children will try to reproduce favorite toys, special belongings, and important people. Their ability to recall is sufficiently developed by now, and they can create these images even when the objects are out of sight. Figures will have bodies and become more and more complete. A figure with one arm or leg larger than the other is not unusual. Big hats on big heads are seen frequently; and more than one object will appear in the same picture. However, the proportions of these objects in relation to each other may remain unrealistic for a while longer. There probably will not be very much movement in the figures, and colors will be chosen more often because they are pleasing rather than because they are realistic.

Artistic skills develop dramatically around the ages of 4 to 7 years. Drawings become more detailed and more realistic. Graphic images progress from telling a simple story about one object at a time to combining several objects in one picture, telling a more elaborate story. Differentiation of male and female, completion of figures, ground lines, more realistic colors, and the influence of culture and environment should be evident by the end of this stage/sequence and before the child can move on to the next level of development.

The ages between 4 and 7 are a critical period of development for children. During this time they finally master their bodily functions and begin to realize the differences between girls and boys. Learning how to relate to more than one adult at a time now occurs, as little girls naturally want to be "Daddy's girl" and little boys want Mommy for themselves. These are normal wishes that will be reflected first in drawings that differentiate between the sexes. Drawing themselves as "big" as a parent is another way for children to fulfill their fantasies through creative expression. Artistic expressions showing three forms, whether objects or people, are produced over and over by children everywhere around these ages. This is one of many ways they begin to work through the normal process of imitating, and then identifying with, a parent of the same sex. It is believed that this identification must be accomplished successfully in order for children to adapt to school and new adult authority figures (teachers), and to form peer relationships.

From ages 7 to 11, children's artwork will tell us how successful they have been in their developmental tasks. Regardless of artistic talent, creative expressions will be rich with fantasies and facts these child artists are accumulating about the world around them. Cultural and ethnic influences will be depicted realistically or symbolically. Such emotions as love, hate, anger, and compassion will be seen through subject matter and the stories children tell in their art productions. Feelings of security and self-confidence will be manifested in the growing awareness and progressive illustrations of realistic proportions of objects in relation to each other, realistic colors, baselines, and horizon lines.

As the child's knowledge of the world expands around the ages of 7 to 11 years, objects in the surroundings are depicted more realistically in art productions, regardless of media. Subject matter may be influenced by interactions with family peers, exciting movies, television shows, and books.

Attending to Danger Signals

Graphic images produced by children during this time also will tell us if they are having problems. We can "see" whether these problems are due to learning disabilities, which may have resulted from a physical impairment or an emotional trauma. If a child has mastered developmental tasks and is progressing normally, drawings will show this normal progression. However, if these developmental tasks have not been mastered, warning signals can be identified in drawings.

Danger signals in children's art work appear in many different forms. For example, if a drawing appears to have been made by a 4-year-old child, and we know that child is 7, we should be concerned. Any indication that a child is functioning intellectually or emotionally at an age younger than the chronological age should be explored further.

Shaky lines may indicate a learning problem or anxiety. When these are seen in a number of drawings by the same child, it is time to call for help.

A form repeated over and over suggests that the child is preoccupied with whatever that form symbolizes. This kind of repetition warns us to examine the source of this preoccupation.

We should be aware that a child is under some stress if objects in the same drawing indicate glaringly different age levels of the artist. The same would be true if we saw consecutive drawings in the same medium, produced by the same child, that reflected different age levels.

The presence of floating objects, produced at a time when that child should be aware of ground lines and should be able to tell a story in pictures, alerts us to the need for further evaluation of that child.

Images that are consistently slanted are warning signals that the child could have a learning disability resulting from a perceptual problem.

A child's spontaneous illustration of a particularly violent or tragic event should warn us (**Fig. 8**). It is important to explore why the child feels the need to illustrate such extraordinary subject matter.

Finally, we should question both the intellectual and emotional development of any child past the age of 4 who cannot stay within the boundaries of the paper, or within boundaries created on the paper.

Now that you are able to identify some of the warning signals, how do you use this knowledge? Let us assume that your daughter is in first grade. Based on report cards and written comments by the teacher you are pleased to know that your child is doing well in her venture into grade school. Shortly after the second semester begins, you receive a call from the teacher asking you to meet with her. Every interested parent or caregiver would arrange for this meeting as soon as possible. When our eldest daughter, Bonnie, was in first grade I received such a call. Curious, I immediately arranged for a meeting. This young, sensitive, and caring teacher told me she was very troubled about our child. Although Bonnie was doing well in her schoolwork, the teacher noticed that she spent considerable time gazing into space and seemed inattentive. The teacher thought this indicated some distress, reflecting a lack of attention from her parents. The teacher knew that there were two younger sisters at home.

I was devastated by the teacher's comments—and furious. I did not believe that we were any less attentive to our eldest daughter than to the two younger girls. When I reported the meeting to my husband, a physician, his first response was to arrange for a physical examination. The medical report showed that Bonnie had a sixty percent hearing loss in one ear, apparently due to the development of excess tissue after a tonsillectomy performed a year earlier. Medical treatment corrected the hearing loss in a few months, and Bonnie's gazing into space and inattentiveness naturally stopped.

I recount this incident because it was an important lesson for me as a parent and for our daughter's teacher. The teacher's observation of behavior that seemed inconsistent with school performance told me that she was very much aware of the children—how they did in their school-work and how they acted in the classroom. However, it was presumptuous of her to assume that she knew the reason for our daughter's behavior without gathering more information. At the time this happened, I was not a professional in the mental health field. Today, however, as I instruct mental-health workers and medical personnel, I constantly remind students that normal physical development is fundamental to normal intellectual and emotional growth. Physical traumas must be considered because they, too, will interfere with learning.

Today there are many resources to help us handle problems, but the availability of these resources is not fully known to the public. Parents and teachers alike feel frustrated when they know there is a need for consultation but are not sure which consultant to contact. Neighbors and friends can be helpful only if they have had personal experience with the same problem. Very often the nature of the problem is difficult to determine. Pediatricians and family physicians are qualified professionals, but their role is limited to exploring whether the problem is medical or something that requires the attention of another professional in the field of mental health and education. If the problem is a physical abnormality, the pediatrician or family physician may be your best guide. In all situations, assessing physical well-being is the first step in dealing with any problem.

Once it has been determined that the child has no physical impairments, what is next? How can parents and teachers find the right people to evaluate the problem further and make recommendations to help the child?

We can illustrate some points about the kind of therapist to choose by analyzing the different danger signals and identifying the professionals most qualified to evaluate the suspected problem, other than an art psychotherapist. In the next chapter we will demonstrate how the art psychotherapist can be most helpful in pinpointing specific areas of concern that would require more discriminating test procedures.

Let us suppose that we feel certain a child is drawing on a level lower than the chronological age. A psychologist trained in testing methods could determine whether this child's level of intelligence is compatible with the chronological age. A clinical psychologist or a psychiatrist might be consulted to assess the behavior, and might recommend additional psychological testing to determine whether there are certain emotional disorders.

This same process could be followed for children whose images float in space, show violent content, or are inconsistent within one picture or from one drawing to the next. These danger signals suggest that the child is very likely to be manifesting some emotional stress or disorder. Intellectual functioning should be evaluated to be sure that the child is not mentally retarded to any degree that would impede normal creative expression.

A child who continually draws slanted images, or ignores page or line boundaries, or repeats the same line or shape in all artistic creations, or cannot draw a line that is sure and direct, should be tested for a perceptual problem and a possible learning disorder. Some psychologists specialize in these areas and are professionally qualified to detect such problems.

In Chapter 8 we will discuss Bobby, who repeatedly drew the image of a "gaping mouth" to master his real trauma of a cleft lip and palate. Often there are similar situations in which a repeated image and lack of attention to boundaries does not mean the child has a learning disorder. The art psychotherapist and psychologist trained in testing measures can confirm that the child is normal developmentally and may recommend further examination of the child's behavior by a psychiatrist or clinical psychologist.

When we have information that defines the problem, we are faced with seeking help to provide some form of intervention or treatment. The questions now are where to find professional help and how do we judge whether those professionals are qualified to handle the problem. In the next chapter we will address finding a qualified therapist.

But it is not enough to know what children communicate in their artwork. It is only useful if they are invited and encouraged to continue to express themselves.

In the previous chapters, we offered suggestions for providing an atmosphere that will encourage children to express themselves creatively. Parents and teachers who are sensitive to this natural creative urge in all children can encourage children by providing simple, inexpensive art supplies and a place in which to use them. Most important of all is accepting the art works children produce and displaying these creative efforts. What children produce is an extension of themselves. Rejection of a child's artwork is a rejection of the child.

Providing art materials and a place to use them is not enough to guarantee that children will feel free to express themselves. All of us at one time or another have given our children "double messages." Unwittingly, we will say one thing but convey another in our actions. In Chapter 2 we gave examples of these possible instances, such as saying yes to painting in an inappropriate place, then getting angry over the "mess." It is important to be aware of these responses in all of us. While limit-setting is necessary for mature development, inconsistencies in adult behavior confuses children of all ages.

Parents and teachers alike must remember that small children draw initially to please themselves. Urging them to draw realistically before they are ready inhibits creativity, as does making judgments about their pictures from an adult viewpoint. Encouragement and appreciation of children's artwork should continue beyond the early years, because it is such a natural form of free expression and a socially acceptable way to express feelings that cannot always be acted out in society. Art expression provides a way for growing children to "picture" themselves in different roles—to fantasize about themselves in adult situations. It is also one way to express and sometimes even "contain" feelings that cannot be expressed easily through words.

It is an unfortunate reality that because teachers may be responsible for large numbers of children in a classroom, they may not always be able to allow for individual creative expression. Art materials and space for creative activities traditionally are low-priority items in the budget. We have no immediate answers for this problem, and share the frustrations of preschool, special education, elementary school, and art teachers. Many tell us that they are continually hampered by these barriers to fostering this natural expression—an expression that gives children pleasure and a means to work through problems, while also letting us know how they are growing, intellectually and emotionally. Perhaps parents who are more aware of the importance of creative expression to their children's mental health will be able to make a greater effort to support art expression in the home and also support the efforts of teachers to obtain more resources for creative expression.

Part of this book has addressed the problem of how to attend to warning signals; but parents, teachers, and caregivers must not assume that recognizing a warning signal means that they will be able to interpret the signal's meaning. When a warning signal is recognized, parents and teachers should consult professionals who can evaluate the child to determine whether there is a problem, and if necessary, what kind of intervention or treatment should be considered.

Earlier in this book we discussed the enormous impact of changes in society as a whole. Any creative expression should be viewed as a reflection of the society in which the expression was produced. We mentioned the effect of television on children's earlier awareness of male and female differences. The "stick figure," traditionally learned by most children around age 7, is rarely seen today in children's drawings. In the past, sexual characteristics did not appear in children's images of figures until around age 9 or 10. Today, these characteristics appear as early as 6 or 7 years, stimulated, we believe by exposure to television. The next generation of clinicians will have the opportunity to evaluate the impact of the V Chip being considered for censorship of inappropriate programs for children. They will also learn more about how access to the Internet impacts on children.

Another issue focusing around changing societal norms is what will be the effect of role reversals on the identification process of boys and girls. Today more and more mothers are working outside the home, and there continues to be an enormous increase in the number of single-parent families. Mothers and fathers are assuming roles traditionally assigned to one or the other. It is not surprising today to hear that Daddy cooks and cleans or Mommy changes the tire on the family car. This is a transition period in society, and it is difficult to predict the eventual effects of this role reversal on children. Personally, I do not believe that this change will cause a major global problem. Role reversals have certainly existed in individual family situations many times in the past. How this was perceived by the children depended entirely on how naturally or unnaturally this was accepted by the parents and communicated to the children. There is considerable evidence that this is still true and will be true in the future. As a family therapist, I have learned that the parent who is personally comfortable with taking on the tasks that in the past were performed by a parent of the opposite sex, and who communicates that comfort to the children, remains an appropriate role model for children of the same sex.

Little girls will identify with Mommies who may change car tires, and little boys will identify with Daddies who cook and clean. What will probably change is society's views of what a man or a woman, a "Mommy" or a "Daddy," is supposed to do. We must try to put aside old beliefs and realize that these kinds of role reversals do not change Mommy into Daddy, or vice-versa.

A form of "cancer" in our society confronts and distresses us daily. The physical and sexual abuse of children is a topic that cannot be properly addressed within the scope of this book. However, we know that sometimes children's drawings can provide us with information about these horrible incidents.

First, it must be said that physical and sexual abuse of children is not a new phenomenon. It has always existed, but today the news media have made us much more aware of its occurrence. When directed by qualified professionals, children will draw realistic and/or symbolic representations of abuses they have endured. These expressions are especially useful in helping children to express and deal with these traumatic events.

Unfortunately, small children who have been sexually abused, but not physically hurt in the act, often do not know that the abusing adult did something wrong until they are old enough to learn this from others. Even when they do know it is wrong, they are often afraid to tell about it, especially if the abuser is a close relative.

Art therapists working with children have, for many years, been qualified as an Expert Witness in alleged abuse cases. In 1986, such a case was brought before Judge Sorkow in Family Court in Hackensack, New Jersey. He had no problem accepting the art therapist as an expert witness, but questioned the validity of art therapy as a qualified discipline. I was asked to testify and at the conclusion of my evidence, Judge Sorkow, in an unprecedented decision ruled art therapy as valid as psychology and psychiatry in such cases. The reference for his position paper and subsequent published article pertaining to this decision is listed in the bibliography.

Much research is underway to determine the best ways to identify child abuse as quickly as possible. At present we do not have sufficient information to allow us to say we can "see" evidence of specific physical or sexual abuse in children's free, non-directed drawings. We can see indicators of children at risk in spontaneous drawings, and such drawings have been shown and discussed throughout this book. Recognizing warning signals in drawings, and having a qualified professional person pursue information about the child and the environment, may reveal that some kind of abuse is the source of the signal. In my own experience, using drawings to evaluate children and supervising art therapy students working with children, this has frequently been the case. But, I repeat, the drawings provided, are only indicators that directed us to examine more closely the child's environment before the exact nature of the problem could be determined.

It is our hope that continued research in this area will identify markers of child abuse in drawings that can be interpreted before the damage caused by physical and sexual abuse is irreversible.

We have endeavored to communicate the importance of creative expression as one way parents and teachers can "see" what children are "saying" about themselves—how, through drawings and other artistic productions, we can chart the normal progression of children's intellectual and emotional development and the problems they encounter.

A number of years ago, I was privileged to work with a very sensitive and creative psychiatric nurse. She became familiar with the use of art psychotherapy for severely disturbed adults, and we often discussed how, for many of these patients, it was the first time in years that they were expressing themselves creatively. The following poem, given to me as a gift from this nurse, is her creative expression of the sadness she felt for those who had been inhibited in their own artistic expressions.

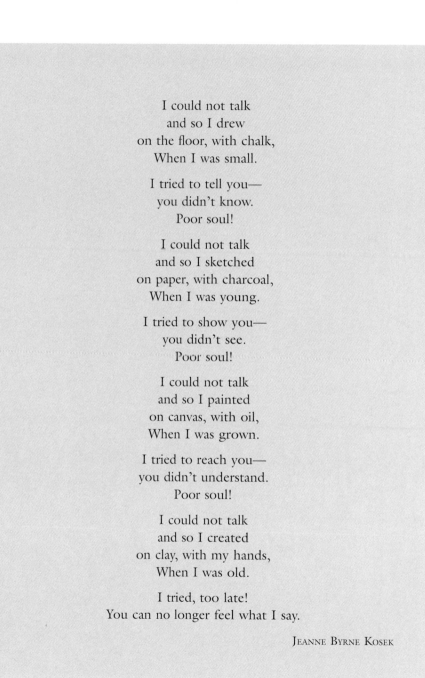

I could not talk
and so I drew
on the floor, with chalk,
When I was small.

I tried to tell you—
you didn't know.
Poor soul!

I could not talk
and so I sketched
on paper, with charcoal,
When I was young.

I tried to show you—
you didn't see.
Poor soul!

I could not talk
and so I painted
on canvas, with oil,
When I was grown.

I tried to reach you—
you didn't understand.
Poor soul!

I could not talk
and so I created
on clay, with my hands,
When I was old.

I tried, too late!
You can no longer feel what I say.

JEANNE BYRNE KOSEK

Chapter 8

What You Can Learn From What I Do

As a member of the helping professions, I know too well that most people do not seek help for themselves or their children until there is a serious problem. Even then the tendency is to deny that there is a problem, until, for whatever reason, dealing with it can no longer be avoided. This kind of denial is normal, but a delay in getting help frequently makes the problem greater. It is not easy to admit that we may need outside help in raising our children.

Sometimes, however, outside help can reassure us that the warning signals in a child's drawings do not indicate a problem that needs intervention. Rather, it may tell us the child has naturally found a way to deal with whatever is a concern. The case of young Bobby will illustrate this point.

Very often, when people learn that I am an art therapist, they will try to test me with a drawing. This occurred a few years ago, when my husband and I met Bobby's grandparents at a resort. After we had known each other for a while and had exchanged the usual bits of information about ourselves and our families, they asked if I would look at some drawings that their 4-year-old grandson had produced. He loved to draw, and they just wanted to know whether he was drawing like other 4-year-olds. After seeing a number of drawings, I realized that this little boy had a real problem. You have already seen an example of Bobby's pictures—**Fig. 15.** In that drawing, produced when he was 3, Bobby included a huge gaping mouth in every image of a face; in fact, this was true of every face he drew. I truthfully told his grandparents that his drawings were like those of other children his age, but that the gaping mouth was a warning signal. I asked whether Bobby was having a problem with his teeth or had sustained an injury to his mouth. The grandparents told me that Bobby had been born with a cleft palate and was in the process of reconstructive surgery.

The most impressive aspect of Bobby's natural creativity is shown in the way he used his drawings to help master and cope with this very real

Figure 150

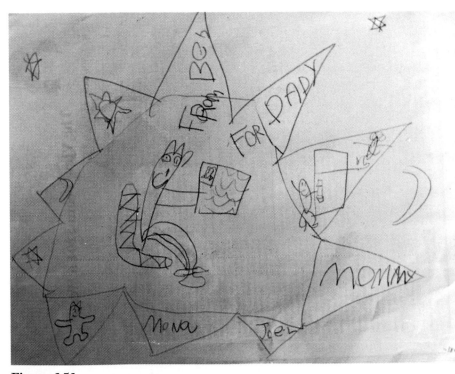

Figure 151

trauma. As surgery was completed, and Bobby had more time to think about other things, such as, school and friends, the faces began to show more realistic proportions. The gaping mouth appeared only occasionally. A "rabbit with whiskers" (produced when Bobby was 3 years, 2 months), and a robot-like face (drawn when he was 4), still show elaboration of detail around the mouth. In **Fig. 150,** which he drew at age 4, Bobby is beginning to combine shapes and lines to create a variety of images, and even to begin to tell a story. At 6, he has created a design out of a star and includes the members of his family (**Fig. 151**). There is no evidence of the gaping mouth.

While visiting his grandparents, Bobby brought me a drawing he had just completed. He has drawn what appears to be a colorful design with two distinctly separate parts. When the picture was turned to the right, the bottom form looked like a gaping mouth with teeth. Before I asked, his grandmother told me Bobby was having trouble with a new tooth. What was so interesting and important was that this trouble was now relegated to only half of the picture rather than dominating it.

In his early pictures, Bobby flashed warning signals by repeating a specific image, over and over. These drawings say that he needed to master his thoughts and feelings about the physical trauma he was experiencing. Drawing the image of a mouth over and over provided a way to do that. Bobby's drawings also show us when that need began to lessen naturally. His most recent image clearly said he can have a problem, even one connected with his mouth, without its becoming the most important thing in his life. Now he can pay attention to other things at the same time. Bobby is lucky. His parents, grandparents, and teachers encourage him to express himself and express some of his growing pains on paper. If we take time to look, Bobby will always tell us how he is progressing. At age 8 he was progressing very well and I learned recently that as a teenager he is participating in a little theatre group.

How The Art Therapist Works

Lori was an above average student in school and had no observable problems. At 10 she was the youngest of four children, with three older brothers aged 14, 16, and 18. Her parents had been receiving marriage counseling for about six months, and I had been supervising their co-therapists, who were student interns in a family therapy program. When the parents expressed concern about one son, I requested an evaluation of the whole family. The parents agreed to participate with their children in a verbal interview by a senior family therapist, as well as an art therapy family evaluation that I conducted, and a movement therapy assessment. The entire evaluation provided information that had remained hidden until that time and allowed us to redirect the focus and course of the parents' therapy sessions. Let us look at what Lori told us.

In the art therapy evaluation, Lori and her family were directed to draw two pictures. The first was to be "anything you want to draw." Lori drew a picture she called "First in line," and said it was "someone who had been first in line, got burned, and was in the hospital" (**Fig. 152**). The person to the right of the figure in bed was a nurse who was also "burned" when she came to help the patient. The second picture that Lori drew was in response to the request to draw a "family picture" (**Fig. 16**). Both of these drawings alerted us to the fact that she was feeling a lot of stress.

We knew that Lori was bright because she has been able to represent one figure so well in the family picture. The inconsistencies in the way she drew other objects, the use of much immature scribbling, the subject matter of someone being first in line and getting burned, and the preoccupation with trash, all communicated to us that she was feeling very disorganized. The fact that Lori was intelligent made it possible for us to help her connect the disorganization in her drawings to the disorder she felt at home. Her parents had insisted that she was too young to know that they were having marital problems. In fact, this child knew more about what was going on

Figure 152

than did her brothers. Lori, who had been trying to maintain order at home by pretending she did not know about her parents' problems, was finally able to release her anxieties on paper with the support of the three therapists. When we explained to her parents what Lori was communicating, they were able to use the guidance of the therapists to re-establish a sense of order and security in their house for all of the children, especially Lori.

Lori's warning signals told us she was feeling considerable emotional stress. In this case, information obtained from the entire family in an extensive evaluation procedure indicated that the parents were not fully aware of their children's feelings. Where the drawings served as documentation for those feelings, they could no longer be denied.

Two children, Rafe, 7 (**Fig. 19**), and Arthur, 6 (**Fig. 14**), were mentioned in Chapter l. Their drawings were identified as examples of warning signals. Both of these boys were students in a school for learning-disabled children. They had difficulty in closing shapes, could not draw recognizable objects, drew slanted forms, and repeated forms and lines. These are all indications of a learning disorder that includes a perceptual problem. The school art therapist described how she worked in that setting with learning disabled children.

Apparently Arthur's problems were not so severe as Rafe's so that with assistance, Arthur could copy shapes. However, it was decided that both boys should be taught basic shapes, such as squares and circles, and should be guided through early developmental drawing sequences. They would be helped to master one sequence before they were introduced to the next. Over a period of several school years, they were given special projects such as shapes to feel and trace. Some of these tasks emerged from discussions with their classroom teacher, so that everyone working with these children was using a consistent approach to helping them learn. Arthur's progress is shown in **Fig. 84**. Rafe's progress is shown in **Fig. 85**.

The relationship of perceptual skills to reading skills is critical, and an art therapist can be a particularly useful member of the team in a school for learning-disabled children. Knowledge of intellectual and emotional development is necessary to work with impaired children, who can learn through art to express feelings related to their problems.

A learning-disabled child may be average or even above-average in intelligence. Sometimes drawings are our first clues to a child's intelligence, because these children cannot learn through traditional classroom methods. In children, the diagnosis of mental retardation, emotional disturbance or learning disability is made on the basis of observation of some form of behavior. In many cases it is very difficult to test these children with traditional psychological procedures. Today we have a new diagnosis, Attention Deficit Disorder (ADD), often accompanied by hyperactivity. And what has been said also holds true with these children.

A number of years ago, I was serving as a consultant to a local school in which some of our art therapy students were working with a class of emotionally disturbed children. At the monthly team meetings—which included the classroom teacher, the school psychologist, the school counselor, the school principal, a representative from the special education department of the Board of Education, and me—we discussed a 7-year-old boy. He had temper tantrums in the classroom and was sometimes unmanageable. We were told that his father was alcoholic, and both his mother and father seemed to have poor parenting skills. However, someone familiar with the family reported that this child was well cared for, was dressed very neatly, and was escorted to the school bus each morning. Nevertheless, our consensus was that he had to be disturbed because of the family history. In these meetings, I was usually asked to review whatever drawings were available, and it was assumed that I would confirm the diagnosis. This was not the case, however. The child's drawings told me that he was having difficulty expressing himself in an organized fashion, and that he had not mastered early developmental sequences. It was possible that this seemingly bright child might be frustrated because he could not learn the way other children did. He knew something was wrong, and his temper tantrums were an expression of this frustration. Further psychological testing for a perceptual problem confirmed what we saw in the drawings. This child was removed from the class for emotionally-disturbed children and entered a class for learning-disabled children, where classroom instruction was specifically designed for these children. Unfortunately, conclusive judgments are too often made on insufficient information and false assumptions. I could not keep the drawings produced by this child, but the next series of drawings reflects a similar situation.

I spent a month working in a preschool in the United Kingdom. The school has a well-qualified staff and is associated with a training center for psychologists that provides consultation if needed. Most of the children in this preschool are from single-parent families or homes in which both parents are employed. Only under unusual circumstances and by special recommendation does the school accept children who are known to have serious emotional problems. The children are admitted as young as 3 if they are toilet-trained. Community law requires all children to be enrolled in a regular accredited school setting by age 5.

During the time I was at the school, problems were diagnosed in three of the ten children. I was not there officially as an art psychotherapist. My plan was to work with "normal" preschoolers in art activities, collecting their drawings for further study. The staff was very cooperative, introducing me as an "art lady" and allowing me the freedom to engage the children in drawing or painting during indoor play. The staff, also aware of my training and experience, invited me to join their weekly meetings.

Michael was 4 years, 10 months old when I arrived at the school, and plans were being made for his entrance into a regular school. He was very articulate but seemed to be aware that he should be able to do certain things better than he did. For example, he could not do puzzles easily unless someone pointed out the colors of the pieces and helped him match them to the picture on the cover of the puzzle box. Michael's frustration over such situations frequently led to explosive behavior. The teachers had assumed that Michael's behavior resulted from his home environment, which was fraught with marital discord. There had been a number of separations and reconciliations between his parents, and at this time his father had been absent from the home for a year. The assumption that Michael's problems reflected his home situation was well founded, and I expected to see evidence of this in Michael's drawings.

What I saw in the first drawing Michael made for me indicated that he was functioning at that time far below a 4- to 5-year-old developmental level. The shaky lines and slant to the form led me to question whether Michael might have a perceptual problem due to minimal brain dysfunction. Michael had been given a standard intelligence test several months earlier, and his emotional problems had been considered when grading this test. The routine evaluations conducted at this school did not include more discriminating testing that could discern the presence of minimal brain dysfunction. To save time, I was asked to do an art therapy evaluation to determine whether there was consistent evidence of the problem I suspected. Knowing Michael's frustration level, I gave him only three tasks. For the usual art therapy evaluation I would use at least five tasks, and possibly six, a standard practice among most trained art therapists.

At my direction, Michael did three drawings: a free drawing that he said was a car (**Fig. 153**); a house that looked like a scribble in a rectangle (**Fig 154**); and a person that he said was a "man who was cross" (**Fig. 155**). Throughout the evaluation process, Michael was aware that the drawings did not look like what he said they were, and he needed much encouragement to complete them. These images confirmed my original suspicions and the consulting psychologist concurred: minimal brain dysfunction. Michael's emotional problems were also evident, particularly in a drawing of his family that is discussed in Chapter 5. The positive result of this evaluation was that Michael's mother, who was undergoing therapy, was able to cope with her own personal stress and do something to help her son. She made arrangements for him to receive tutoring in a specialized school program and to meet a therapist once a week. It is always risky to try to predict the results of any intervention, but it is believed that Michael will do well if this kind of support from mother and school continues.

In contrast, let us consider Brian, who was 4 years, 3 months old when he drew a cement truck (**Fig. 156**) and "Brian crying" (**Fig. 157**). The drawing of the cement truck is very advanced for a child of this age, telling us that Brian is very bright. His intellectual development, as evidenced by the drawing, is closer to a 6-year-old than to a 4-year-old. His truck sits on the ground and is drawn very much like a toy truck he used in play, but that object was not in sight when he drew this.

Brian's drawing of himself tells another story. He does not see himself as a whole person, and he tearfully communicates his fear that he will never be complete. He repeated this same self-image in many drawings. The startling difference between Brian's drawing of an object in his environment and a drawing of himself tells us that intellectually he can represent an object in his environment when he chooses, but that he has a great deal of difficulty reflecting a normal self-image in his drawings. At this early age, this kind of difference between two developmental paths, intellectual and emotional, is a serious warning sign that Brian will not be able to adjust to school and peer relationships. He was not able to play well with other children in the preschool, and his behavior was often unpredictable and strange. In this situation, we all agreed that he was a very disturbed child who would probably require psychotherapy for years. I also learned that

Figure 153

Figure 155

Figure 154

Figure 156

Figure 157

Brian's mother was very disturbed and that an effort was being made to provide treatment for her and her son.

One of the advantages in serving as a consultant to other therapists who have drawings produced by their patients or clients is that I am sometimes able to discuss these drawings in my writings. Jenny's two drawings came to me in this manner. Her therapist is a psychologist and registered music therapist. A well-trained clinician who knows that all children like to draw, she encourages creative expression in a variety of media. Jenny drew a self-portrait at age 8 shortly after she was referred for therapy **(Fig. 158)**. The way she has drawn this figure indicates that she is able to represent people on an intellectual and artistic level appropriate for her age. The image suggests fear and anger. We have learned that when children are abused they often draw themselves in very aggressive images, not unlike the person they perceive as the abuser. There was some concern in this case that Jenny was abused and drawing herself like her mother. The figure is floating and filled in with very agitated lines.

A year later, Jenny spontaneously drew another portrait of herself **(Fig. 159)**. Her therapist was struck by similarities and differences between these two images. Jenny is clearly on the ground, the fierce mouth is replaced by a smile, feminine eyelashes and flying pigtails replace the glaring eyes and jagged hair, and the upraised arms support a jump rope. In this second drawing we can see that Jenny is not feeling as angry and afraid as she had been a year before. This new drawing supported what Jenny's therapist noted in her behavior. She was a much calmer, happier child who was beginning to be able to function in a much healthier way in school and at home.

On a rare occasion I am not able to keep the pictures I have evaluated. Such was the case with a drawing brought to me by a police officer investigating a series of murders. It seemed that one of the victims, a young teen-

Figure 158   Figure 159

ager and a relative of the murderer, had drawn a sad and disturbing picture of a little boy in a cage calling for help. He gave the picture to his teacher, who did not know what to do with it, but kept it. When the police questioned people who knew the murder victims, the teacher showed them the picture, produced months before the child was killed. He was calling for help, but the teacher did not see what he was saying. It is impossible to say that, if the teacher had known this was really a cry for help, she could have prevented the child's murder. But we can say that we cannot afford to neglect what children draw. More and more the courts are paying attention. For many years I have been asked to evaluate children and parents in custody cases, with drawings submitted as evidence on behalf of the children's interests. In addition, a growing awareness of the value of nonverbal communication in drawings has called me to the courtroom as an expert witness in criminal cases. Similar instances have occurred with colleagues throughout the country. And in Chapter 7, I discussed the utilization of drawings as evidence in cases of alleged abuse.

It is obvious that with more and more opportunities becoming available, art therapists generally tend to be selective in the populations they choose to work with. While much of my professional work has been in the area of training clinicians, my major area of interest and research has been child development and early intervention. My fantasy is to stand on a soap box wherever I lecture or serve as a consultant and tell everyone they must pay attention to children's drawings so that we may be able to help a child before a problem is manifest in overt behavior or severe learning difficulties. I am not alone, but one of the difficulties facing art therapists (and other clinicians) is the limited training in developing credible evaluation instruments. While serving as a consultant to the Dade County (FL) School System, I gained the support of the administration and the (then) eleven members of the Clinical art therapy staff to develop an art therapy assessment looking at the relationship between emotional and cognitive development. This process was spearheaded by the director of that program, Janet Bush. Having heard my soap-box oratory as a student in my training program, she recognized the need for a uniform evaluation procedure among her staff and was able to implement the structure to formulate what is now known as the Levick Emotional and Cognitive Art Therapy Assessment (LECATA). This instrument is based on my text, They Could Not Talk and So They Drew (1983) and examines intellectual development and coping mechanisms identified in drawings. It was copyrighted in 1989, and is used throughout the Dade County School by the twenty-one art therapists now employed there. Ms. Bush and I conduct seminars to train art therapists in the use of this tool, and members of this discipline (trained in our seminars) are now utilizing the LECATA throughout the country. Plans for a normative study and publication of a manual are in process.

This evaluation consists of six tasks, all designed to provide specific information about what level of development that the child taking the test is functioning. We have had encouraging feedback from our colleagues and continue to work to refine this assessment. While the scope of this evaluation is beyond this book, and a report is very lengthy, the following are examples of a single-task drawing from three children to illustrate the potential and value of early assessment.

Jamie was 5 years old and in kindergarten. Her teacher raised some concern as to whether or not Jamie should move on to first grade. Her parents, believing she was ready, requested an evaluation. In drawing the picture of herself, the second task **(Fig. 160)**, Jamie drew a figure, including all the features and parts. She added lines coming down from top of the head and told me it was a special picture of her with hair very long and below her feet. She signed her name and asked me to write the description. This image is on a 5-year level intellectually, and Jamie is aware that this is not how her hair really looks. The entire series of drawings documented that Jamie functioned on an age-appropriate level, intellectually as well as emotionally, and should be promoted to first grade. This evaluation was presented to the school and validated by information from the school psychologist. We did learn that Jamie is a very curious child and may not always be willing to conform to demands. We recommended she be encouraged to learn how to postpone some of her own wishes and needs when there are other demands she must respond to. Jamie is in fourth grade now and doing very well.

Jimmy was 11 years old when his father called, concerned that his son had told him he was not happy and did not have many friends. We scheduled an evaluation that was conducted shortly after his father's call. At the time, my studio was arranged so that as Jimmy did his self-portrait he was sitting in front of a glass window reflecting his image. Throughout this task, he repeatedly studied himself in the glass and the self-portrait is amazingly like him **(Fig. 161.)** The drawing clearly indicates his age appropriate intellectual ability and at the same time captures his early adolescent awkwardness and sense of being ungrounded. This, no doubt, contributed to

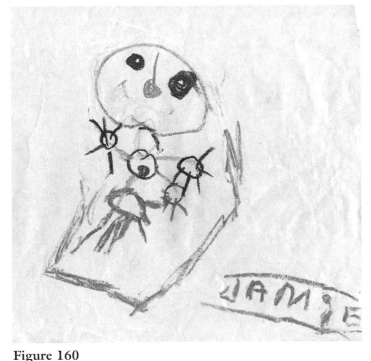

Figure 160

Figure 161

his feeling of being isolated from his peers, and he articulated he did not know how to cope with this. His other drawings confirmed that Jimmy was in the pre-adolescent stage and not very comfortable with the changes he was experiencing physically and emotionally. From the history, and his drawing of his family, it became apparent that some circumstances within the family needed to be addressed. In consultation with his parents, they acknowledged these problems, were willing to confront them, and were sensitive to changes that needed to be made to help Jimmy develop a better self-image and social skills. I did not see Jimmy again until he was 16 years old. He called to ask if he could interview me for a school project, and of course I agreed. A tall attractive young man arrived, looking very different from the Jimmy I had met at 11. He presented an air of confidence and told me about his interests, his friends, and his plans for college. Jimmy is lucky. His parents paid attention to what he said, heard what they saw in the drawings he did in my office and followed through.

One of the tasks in the LECATA is to do a scribble and to make a picture out of it. This task is designed to assess a child's ability to solve a problem in a variety of ways. Lisa, at 7, did not have any problems, but with the consent of her parents, offered to serve as a subject for this evaluation. Lisa did a small scribble in green Cray-pas, then used pink to make a face and hat **(Fig. 162)**. She called it "My Big Mexican Fatso," and it does indeed look like a roly-poly figure with a Mexican hat on.

At 7, Lisa is able to abstract an image from a scribble in a humorous and cartoon-like style, telling us she is functioning intellectually several years ahead of her chronological age. Her other images supported this, and our conclusions were not wrong. At 12, Lisa excels in all of her class work and is involved in many school activities with her peers.

Watching children grow through their creative expressions is like watching a film progress, frame by frame. And if one of the frames suggests a problem, there are resources where help can be found to address the problem. I am still on my soap box and ask parents, teachers, and caregivers to join me. Invite your children to feel free to express themselves. And see what they say.

Figure 162

Afterword

The Foundations of Art Therapy

In the Introduction I emphasized that any form of art production contains a nonverbal message about the artist/creator's inner self and external world. Acceptance of the fact that children's art expressions do have meaning is the first step in learning to look, listen, and respond to what our children are telling us.

Professionals in the field of mental health have recognized the magnitude of nonverbal communication for many years. Movement/dance therapists have taught us that body language can summon joy as well as a feeling of devastating rejection. The power of music therapy is cited in the Bible: King Saul was told to have someone play the lyre for him when he felt tormented. Observing a music therapist playing the piano and connecting with the rocking rhythm of an autistic child is an extraordinary experience. Art-making as a significant nonverbal communication was first described by psychiatrists in 1912. They began to recognize the value of drawings in diagnosing emotional problems. Gradually the importance of collecting information about the artist along with the drawings formed the basis for the first component of art therapy—diagnosis.

It is important to repeat that this book is not intended to make readers art therapists, a trained professional, qualified to examine the artwork of children and adults who may be struggling with conflicts between their inner and outer worlds. The goal of the book is to provide information that will aid parents, teachers, and caregivers to chart the normal development of their children through their drawings and to alert them to breaks, gaps or deviations in that chart. To help these people better understand how creative expression can be therapeutic, information about the field of art therapy is provided.

The art therapist observes the creative expression, and unlike the early proponents of art expression as an indicator of diagnoses, seeks information to substantiate a diagnosis. Only after securing appropriate information does the art therapist begin actual treatment: the use of art to help heal emotional stress. Among art therapists, there are two schools of thought— "Art as Therapy" and "The Art in Therapy." The "Art as Therapy" approach assumes that the very act of creating something artistic (and this includes music and dance) is healing. Any expression of art can be a way to obtain pleasure, release tension, or express anger. Just stop for a moment and think. Do you doodle, sing in the shower, or start dancing when you hear music? If you do not, it may be because somewhere along the path of growing up you became inhibited. As we have said many times before, all children do these things naturally.

This "Art as Therapy" approach emerged in the 1930s and 1940s, when a small group of artists began working with mental patients in hospitals and with problem children in residential treatment centers. Most of these artists were invited into these settings by administrators and psychiatrists, who believed that some form of art activity would be very beneficial to these patients. It was not very long before these artists were being called art therapists. Their writings tell us how, after drawing, sculpting, or painting, patients exhibited diminished symptoms.

The other approach, "Art in Therapy," also emerged in the 1930s and 1940s. This group of art therapists began to examine the drawings of disturbed children and adults for clues as to what they were saying about themselves consciously, and to elicit associations that would help the therapist determine what the artist/creators were saying about themselves unconsciously. The goal of these art therapists was very similar to the goals of psychoanalysts who encourage patients to discuss dreams and childhood memories. Many art therapists and other mental health professionals began to realize that the artist, whether the patient was a child or adult, normal or abnormal, produced images that could be likened to having a dream in a waking state. Helping the artist become aware of all the parts of the image, and of the thoughts and feelings that produced that image, was a new and provocative approach to revealing hidden feelings and thoughts. Sometimes these thoughts and feelings were revealed after traditional psychotherapeutic practices had failed to disclose them.

Since the early 1960s, the field of art therapy has grown rapidly. A national governing body, The American Art Therapy Association (AATA) was established in 1968, and there are more than 4,000 registered art therapists. The difference between an art therapist and an art psychotherapist is only a difference in practice; practitioners in both categories qualify for professional registration by AATA. Formal training programs are now available all over the country. In order to obtain professional standing, the AATA recommends that applicants possess an undergraduate degree with a major in the fine arts or art education, and graduate training in art therapy.

As the number of art therapists/psychotherapists has grown, there have been many contributions to the literature about art therapy. These many books and articles have helped to sharpen our skills, broaden our scope, and develop more comprehensive training programs. Years of experience have also led us to search continually for new ways to use our knowledge and skills and for new ways to describe to others in related professions how to "hear" what we see.

A few art therapists continue to adhere to either the "Art as Therapy" or the "Art in Therapy" approach. Many more have become sensitive to the fact that some individuals benefit more from one approach than from the other, and more often mix the two approaches. The qualified art therapist today is able to provide the best means of artistic expression for a particular patient, regardless of which approach is recommended.

Art therapists have learned to blend art skills with different psychological theories, and many are members of treatment teams including psychiatrists, psychologists, social workers, teachers, nurses, and other physicians. Sometimes the art therapist is responsible only for conducting an evaluation and imparting information about the evaluation to others who are directing a course of intervention or treatment. At other times, art therapists actually direct and conduct the intervention or treatment based on conclusions reached jointly with other mental health professionals.

The first small group of art therapists evolved an identity for their specialty by working with psychiatrists in hospital settings for very disturbed mental patients and residential schools for problem children. Today, art therapists work in public and private schools with normal, abnormal, and handicapped children, and in prisons, inpatient units in hospitals, outpatient clinics, day-care centers, and nursing homes. Art therapists help prepare children for surgery and other hospital procedures, work with patients receiving dialysis for kidney disease, and provide counseling for children and adults faced with the physical and mental trauma of terminal illness. Medical breakthroughs have added years to the life span, and art therapists are working with senior citizens in nursing homes, retirement homes, and in private practice. In all of these situations, the artistic expression provides another way for that child or adult to cope with an illness, a loss, or adjustment to change, and to express feelings that might otherwise remain hidden. It is the hidden, suppressed feelings and thoughts that cause symptoms that are a call for help.

Some art therapists have private practices, some have become family therapists, and some have become licensed professionals in other areas of mental health. Regardless of career direction, the crucial qualification of the successful art therapist is the individual ability to work creatively to mesh art skills with an in-depth knowledge of nonverbal communication, and psychological constructs.

About the Author

Myra F. Levick postponed pursuing her own art career to work while her husband attended medical school. In 1958, when their third and youngest daughter was in second grade, her husband encouraged Dr. Levick to resume her studies, and she obtained a Bachelor of Fine Arts degree (B.F.A.) from Moore College of Art in Philadelphia.

Dr. Levick planned to continue graduate study for a master's degree in the history of art. However, she became intrigued by the idea, proposed by the late Morris J. Goldman, M.D., of working in the psychiatric unit at the Albert Einstein Medical Center, Northern Division, a general hospital in Philadelphia. Dr. Goldman, the director of this unit, was convinced of the value of having an artist work with mentally ill patients. While Dr. Levick employed her art skills in working with the patients, she also studied psychiatry and psychology, obtaining a master's degree in educational psychology (M.Ed.) from Temple University in Philadelphia.

During this time, Dr. Levick and Dr. Goldman, along with Paul J. Fink, M.D., a psychoanalyst on the Einstein staff, published journal articles about their experiences in art therapy, stimulating the interests of art students, art teachers, and practicing artists to pursue training in this growing field. By 1967 Dr. Fink, who had become director of education in the department of psychiatry at Hahnemann Medical College and Hospital (later Hahnemann University, now Allegheny University of the Health Sciences) in Philadelphia, and Dr. Goldman, who had become director of the Hahnemann Mental Health Community Center, convinced the graduate school of that institution to initiate the first program anywhere offering graduate-level training leading to a master's degree in art therapy.

Dr. Levick joined this group at Hahnemann and with the support of specialists in child psychology, psychiatrists, and educators in the community, the program was offered to a continually growing student body in a variety of settings. Attracting the interest of practicing art therapists all over the country, a guest lecture series and meeting for these practitioners was sponsored by Hahnemann in 1968. This led to the establishment of The American Art Therapy Association (AATA), which approves training programs and registers art therapists. Dr. Levick was elected its first president.

Dr. Levick studied family and group psychotherapy in the early 1970s, and she became a licensed psychologist, in Pennsylvania, with a specialty in art psychotherapy. She continued to study psychology, maintaining a private clinical practice along with her academic position at Hahnemann, which included teaching and supervising creative arts therapy students, family therapy students, psychology students and medical psychiatric residents.

In 1976 Dr. Levick was asked to design and coordinate a program at Hahnemann to provide training for art, dance/movement, and music therapists. Initially supported by a three-year grant from the National Institute of Mental Health, this became the model program in this country, for training creative arts therapists together in a graduate program within a medical school. Dr. Levick was named director of the program, called the Master's Creative Arts in Therapy Program (MCAT), and she became a professor in the Department of Mental Health Sciences and in the medical college.

At the same time, Dr. Levick continued her own academic pursuits, receiving a Ph.D. in child development and education from Bryn Mawr College in 1981. In 1984, seeking more time to work on her second book, she relinquished her title as Director of MCAT at Hahnemann, remaining in her current capacity as professor and consultant to the program.

Dr. Levick's textbook, *They Could Not Talk and So They Drew: Children's Styles of Coping and Thinking*, was published in 1982, and the investigative work for that textbook became the basis for *Mommy, Daddy, Look What I'm Saying*, and the development of the *Levick Emotional and Cognitive Art Therapy Assessment* (LECATA). Dr. Levick has authored numerous scholarly articles and book chapters. She served as president of AATA from 1969 to 1971, has long been a member of the executive board of the Association, and was named an honorary life member in 1973. She is Editor-in-Chief Emeritus of an international professional journal, *The Arts in Psychotherapy*, and continues to be a guest lecturer and teacher all over the world.

Her home is now in Boca Raton, Florida, where she is the Director of the South Florida Art Psychotherapy Institute. Through the office of this Institute, Dr. Levick conducts annual training seminars on the use of the LECATA and offers consultation and supervision to clinicians in the field of mental health. Dr. Levick maintains a small private practice in art psychotherapy, and at this writing, she is also president of the board of directors of a local community day school, kindergarten through eighth grade.

Appendix

Sources of Professional Help

What You Need to Know

You can call local colleges or universities and inquire whether they have programs in art therapy, psychology, or social work. If they do, they will undoubtedly have clinics that provide evaluation services. Hospitals and medical schools may provide similar facilities. School districts generally employ school psychologists and counselors and may be able to provide the necessary evaluation. It is your responsibility as a parent or a care giver to check the credentials of someone who is going to guide you in helping your child. It is also your right.

The educational requirements of an *art psychotherapist*, as well as the way in which training programs are monitored, have been previously described. The accrediting body for a *psychologist* is the American Psychological Association. This association accredits programs training psychologists. Licensing requirements for psychologists vary from state to state. Most states require rigorous training and supervision in both clinical and testing proficiency, in addition to a doctoral degree—a Psy.D. or a Ph.D. In some states a psychologist with a master's degree can become licensed and thus be eligible for third party payments. Traditionally, the psychologist, who does not have a medical degree, could not prescribe medication. In recent years, a course in psychotherapeutic drugs has been available to psychologists who want this privilege.

A *psychiatrist* is a graduate physician (medical doctor or doctor of osteopathy) who has completed at least three years of specialty training in psychiatry after completing medical school.

A *psychoanalyst* must first be a psychiatrist and then complete additional training and undergo psychoanalysis with a "training analyst". Psychiatrists become certified under the jurisdiction of the American Board of Psychiatry and Neurology. The psychiatrist and psychoanalyst, as physicians, can prescribe medication.

A *school psychologist/counselor* may have a background in social work, psychology, or a related field of study. In this field also, state requirements for qualifications, certification, or licensing are not consistent.

Choosing a clinic to provide the help you seek presents issues you must address. For example, you should question the staff composition—will the child be evaluated by a qualified graduate staff person or an intern? It is acceptable to have an evaluation, by an intern providing the intern is supervised closely by a recognized professional. What is the philosophy and orientation of the director of the clinic? Is treatment based on drug therapy that alleviates symptoms, psychotherapy that focuses on the source of the problem, or a combined approach that is open and sensitive to the needs of the patients? An advantage to obtaining help from a clinic affiliated with a hospital of a medical school is that these institutions increasingly favor a team approach, in which professionals from several different specialties are involved in diagnosis and treatment. This can be extremely effective, especially if the problem involves an organic impairment, such as minimal brain dysfunction, and an emotional disorder that is functional.

Usually, an evaluation is followed by intervention or treatment. The person or persons who perform the evaluation will designate which professional(s) will direct and/or carry out the recommended procedure. A special school may be recommended for the child who is mentally retarded or has a learning disability. Therapists suggested may include psychologists, psychiatrists, or art, dance/movement, music, family or group therapists.

It is your prerogative to question *why* a particular form of treatment is chosen and *why* a particular therapist is consulted. The credentials of a therapist should be reviewed in the same manner in which you pursued that information in selecting someone to evaluate your child.

Information about the availability of assessment and treatment facilities in your community can also be obtained from a state or county department of health. Each state has an agency that provides both physiological and psychological evaluations of children.

A federal law, Public Law 94-142, the Education for All Handicapped Children Act of 1975 was amended in 1986 and 1990. It is up for reauthorization in 1997. It has been folded into the Individual Disability Act of 1990. However, the provisions originally included remain. They are:

1. to assure that all handicapped children have available to them a free appropriate public education;
2. to assure that the rights of the handicapped children and their parents are protected;
3. to assist States and localities to provide for the education of handicapped children; and
4. to assess and assure the effectiveness of efforts to educate such children.

If your child requires special tutoring, intervention, or treatment, this law requires that county and state public education systems provide the recommended tutors or therapists. A copy of the current status of this law can be obtained from your state board of education.

To insure competent diagnosis and treatment for your child, you should try to avoid the advice of well-meaning, but untrained friends and relatives. Explore the available resources in your community, and if necessary, write to the appropriate state or national office for further information. Be sure to check credentials beyond education alone; experience in treating other children with the same problem as your child's is critical. An individual may have impeccable qualifications, but little or no experience in addressing certain problems.

How and Where to Find Help

The following list of facilities, professionals, and organizations has been prepared to guide you in seeking help when you see a warning signal in your child's creative expressions. Your options may be determined by the availability of qualified people in your community.

Many professional associations publish journals that contain case histories of children with particular problems; these journals are available in many libraries. Those readers familiar with computers and the Internet have at their fingertips many references. For the reader who wishes to learn more, the Bibliography also includes the titles of books about the creative arts in therapy and about developmental psychology. Parents and teachers must be cautioned, however, not to apply this information without professional guidance.

Books that suggest art activities may be found in hobby and toy shops and libraries. It is recommended that you avoid books in which the projects described limit and inhibit free creative expression for the normal child. Craft kits and coloring books are examples of restrictive art activities. Creative ventures for the emotionally-disturbed or learning-disabled child should be guided by a qualified art therapist or other specialists in this area of mental health and education.

Facilities
    Clinics in hospitals and medical schools
    Private clinics
    State clinics
    Clinics associated with colleges and universities that offer specialized programs in psychology, the arts in therapy, and related fields
    Public schools

Professional Personnel
    Pediatrician
    Family physician
    Clinical psychologist
    School psychologist
    Psychologist who specializes in testing procedures
    Psychiatrist
    Psychoanalyst
    Art psychotherapist
    Speech therapist
    Dance/movement therapist
    Music therapist
    Occupational therapist

Organizations

American Art Therapy Association
1202 Allanson Road
Mundelein, IL 60060
E-mail: estygariii.aol.com

American Dance Therapy
Association
2000 Century Plaza, Suite 108
Columbia, MD 21044
E-mail: ADTA@aol.com

American Association For
Music Therapy
1 Station Plaza
Ossing, NY 10562

American Medical Association
535 N. Dearborn Street
Chicago, IL 60610

American Psychiatric Association
1700 18th Street, NW
Washington, DC 20009

American Psychological Association
122 17th Street, NW
Washington, DC 20036
    Division 16: School
    psychology
    E-mail: JBAKER
    @uga.cc.uga.edu

National Institute of Health (NIH)
Bethesda, MD 20892

Information pertaining to all
government health agencies
available at this address; and
http/www.nimh.nih.gov/

U.S. Department of Education
400 Maryland Avenue, SE
Washington, DC 20202

Bibliography

Alshuler, R. H., and L. W. Hattwick. *Painting and Personality.* Chicago: University of Chicago Press, 1947 (rev. ed., 1969).

Arnheim, R. *Art and Visual Perception.* Berkeley: University of California Press, 1954 (rev. ed., 1974).

Arnheim, R. *Visual Thinking.* Berkeley: University of California Press, 1969.

Axline, V. M. *Dibs in Search of Self.* Boston: Houghton Mifflin, 1966.

Bettelheim, B. *Love Is Not Enough.* Illinois: The Free Press, 1950.

Bruner, J. S. "The Course of Cognitive Growth." *American Psychologist* 19 (1964): 1–15.

Coles, R. *Erick Erikson, The Growth of His Work.* Boston: Little Brown, 1970.

Decarie, T. Goyin. *Intelligence and Affectivity in Early Childhood.* New York: International Universities Press, 1965.

DiLeo, J. H. *Young Children and Their Drawings.* New York: Bruner/Mazel, 1970.

DiLeo, J. H. *Children's Drawings as Diagnostic Aids.* New York: Bruner/Mazel, 1973.

Fink, P. J., M. J. Goldman, and M. F. Levick, "Art Therapy, A New Discipline." *Pennsylvania Medicine* 70 (1967):60–66.

Fraiberg, S. *The Magic Years.* New York: Charles Scribner Sons, 1959.

Freud, A. "Normality and Pathology in Childhood: Assessments of Development." *The Writings of Anna Freud.* Vol. 6. New York: International Universities Press, 1965.

Furth, H. G. *Thinking Without Language.* Englewood Cliffs, N.J.: Prentice-Hall, 1966.

Gantt, L., and M. Strauss. *Art Therapy—A Bibliography, January 1940–June 1973.* National Institute of Mental Health, 1974.

Gardner, H. *The Arts and Human Development.* New York: John Wiley and Sons, 1973.

Greenspan, S. I. "Intelligence and Adaptation." In *Psychological Issues,* edited by H. J. Schlesinger. New York: International Universities Press, Inc., 1979, 12, 3/4.

Haber, R. N. "Where Are the Visions in Visual Perception?" In *Imagery—Current Cognitive Approaches,* edited by S. J. Segal. New York: Academic Press, 1971, 36–48.

Hammer, E. F. *The Clinical Application of Projective Drawing.* 2d ed. Springfield, Ill: Charles C. Thomas, 1978.

Hardiman, G. W., and T. Zernich. "Some Considerations of Piaget's Cognitive-Structuralist Theory and Children's Artistic Development." *Studies in Art Education* 23 (1980):3.

Horowitz, M. J. *Image Formation and Cognition.* New York: Appleton-Century-Crofts, 1970.

Inhelder, B., and J. Piaget. *The Growth of Logical Thinking From Childhood to Adolescence.* Translated by A. Parsons and S. Milgram. New York: Basic Books, 1958 (originally published, 1955).

Kellogg, R. with S. O'Dell. *The Psychology of Children's Art.* CRM—Random House Publication, 1967.

Kellogg, R. *Analyzing Children's Art.* Palo Alto, California: Mayfield Publishing Co., 1969, 1970.

Kestenberg, J. S. *Children and Parents: Psychoanalytic Studies in Development.* New York: Jason Aronson, 1975.

Koppitz, E. M. *Psychological Evaluation of Children's Human Figure Drawings.* New York: Grune & Stratton, 1968.

Kramer, E. *Art Therapy in a Children's Community.* Springfield, Ill.: Charles C. Thomas, 1958.

Kwiatkowska, H. *Family Therapy and Evaluation Through Art.* Springfield, Ill.: Charles C. Thomas, 1978.

Lewis, M. M. *Language, Thought, and Personality.* New York: Basic Books, 1963.

Levick, M. (1986) *Mommy, Daddy, Look What I'm Saying: What Children Are Telling Through Their Drawings.* M. Evans. NY.

Levick, M. et al. *Levick Emotional and Cognitive Art Therapy Assessment.* © 1989. In process.

Levick, M. F. "The Goals of the Art Therapist as Compared to Those of the Art Teacher." *Journal of Albert Einstein Medical Center* 15 (1967):157–170.

Levick, M. F. "Family Art Therapy in the Community." *Philadelphia Medicine* 69 (1973):257–261.

Levick, M. F. "Art in Psychotherapy." In *Current Psychotherapies,* edited by J. Masserman. New York: Grune & Stratton, 1975.

Levick, M. F. *They Could Not Talk and So They Drew.* Springfield, Ill.: Charles C. Thomas, 1983.

Levick, M. F., and J. Herring. "Family Dynamics—As Seen Through Art Therapy." *Art Psychotherapy* 1 (1973):45–54.

Levick, M. F., D. Dulicai, C. Briggs, and I. Billock. "The Creative Arts Therapies." In *A Handbook for Specific Learning Disabilities,* edited by W. Adamson and K. Adamson. New York: Gardner Press, 1979.

Levick, M; Safran, D; and Levine, A. (1989). Art therapists as expert witnesses: A judge delivers a precedent-setting decision. *The Arts in Psychotherapy.* Vol. 16.

Lowenfeld, V. *Creative and Mental Growth.* 3rd ed. New York: Macmillan, 1957.

Machover, K. *Personality Projection in the Drawing of the Human Figure.* 2d ed. Springfield, Ill.: Charles C. Thomas, 1978.

Mahler, M., F. Pine, and A. Bergman. *The Psychological Birth of the Human Infant.* New York: Basic Books, 1975.

Naumburg, M. *Studies of Free Art Expression in Behavior of Children as a Means of Diagnosis and Therapy.* New York: Coolidge Foundation, 1947.

Odier, C. *Anxiety and Magical Thinking.* New York: International Universities Press, 1956.

Piaget, I. *Play, Dreams, and Imitation in Childhood.* Translated by C. Gattegno and F. M. Hodgson. New York: W. W. Norton, 1962 (originally published, 1946).

Rosen, H. *Pathway to Piaget.* Cherry Hill, New Jersey: Postgraduate International, 1977.

Rubin, J. A. *Child Art Therapy.* New York: Van Nostrand, Reinhold, 1978.

Sorkow, J.S.C., P.J.F.P. (1986) *Wilkerson vs. Pearson.* Chancery Division. Superior Court of New Jersey.

Winnicott, D. W. *Playing and Reality.* New York: Basic Books, 1971.

Index

Abused children, 107, 108, 118
Adolescence, 87, 91, 99, 101, 113, 120
Adults, 125
Age level inconsistencies (in drawings), 43, 78, 85, 95, 96, 97, 103, 113, 116
American Art Therapy Association (AATA), 124, 128
American Board of Psychiatry & Neurology, 130
American Psychological Association, 129
Anxieties, 45, 79, 87, 103, 114
Art psychotherapists, *See* Art therapists
Art supplies, 20, 22, 106
Art therapists, 19, 41, 53, 85, 97, 105, 108, 111, 113, 123–25, 131
Art therapy, 113, 121
Art therapy, theories of, 124
Assessment, 23, 35, 85, 100, 101, 105, 113, 114, 115, 116, 119, 120, 123, 129, 130

Babble-scribble stage/sequence, 6, 11, 22, 25, 26, 31
Behaviors (of children), 26, 34, 35, 37, 39, 47, 54, 55, 63, 67, 73, 86–87, 101, 102, 105, 116, 118
Boundaries, 27, 33, 84, 104

Children at risk, 108
Circles, 31
Clinics, choosing, 131
Clowns, 50
Color, 35
    See Paint
Control, 22, 27
    See Boundaries, paint
Consultants, 105, 106, 118, 119
Counselors, school, 129, 130
Court decision, 108

Creativity, 1, 19, 23, 24, 41, 64, 106, 107
    barriers, 19, 106
    environment, 22, 123
Cultural influences, 10, 32, 80, 102, 107

Danger signals, *See* Warning signals
Denial, 32
Developmental labs, 10, 17, 28, 43, 44, 96, 101
Diagnosis, *See* assessment
Displaying of art, 20
Divorce, 47, 107

Education for All, Handicapped Children Act of 1975, 130
Emotional development, 1, 20, 34, 38, 54, 102, 104, 114
Environmental (creative), 21
    home, 15, 32, 36, 44, 70, 108, 113
    school, 21
Evaluation, *See* Assessment
Expert witness, 108, 119

Fact-fantasy stage/sequence, 15, 16, 63–97
Family
    in drawings, 8, 9, 17, 41, 46, 56, 57, 60, 67, 68, 80
Fantasies, 15, 21, 24, 32, 37, 42, 47, 53, 58, 59, 65, 66, 73, 92, 93, 94, 97, 103, 106
Fine motor control, 28
Finger painting, 22
Floating foams, 8, 54, 60, 67, 72, 95, 104, 105, 118, 120
Forms
    outline, 12, 22
    repetition, 8, 61,62
    realistic, 40, 47, 49, 51, 59
    See also Floating forms

Graffiti
Ground lines, 7, 49, 59, 63, 67, 68, 76, 77, 88, 90, 91, 96, 97

Halloween, 60, 74, 99
Hospitalization, 43, 100
Human figures, 7, 8, 10, 13, 14, 17, 35, 39, 43, 47, 55, 88, 89, 90, 95, 102, 118
Hyperactive children, 84, 85, 114

Identification, 63, 66, 80, 88, 89, 91, 103, 107
Images, visual, 1, 3, 10, 13, 17, 20, 34, 39, 102, 124
    See also Forms
Imbalance, feeling, 51, 52, 55, 66
Imitating, 22, 34, 37, 38
Imaginary friends
    See Fantasy
Independence, 66
Individual Disability Act of 1990, 130
Individual freedom, 62
    separate, 32, 55
Intelligence, 11, 39, 54, 60, 87, 113, 114
    and artistic expression, 10, 17, 25, 80, 89–93, 102
Intervention, See Treatment

Language, See Verbal development
Learning-disabled children, 22, 46, 62, 72, 84, 96, 100, 103–105, 114, 115, 116
Levick Emotional and Cognitive Art Therapy Assessment (LECATA), 119–121

Mastery, 42, 43, 48, 58, 61, 71, 72, 101, 103, 111, 114
Mental health, 2, 19, 104, 106, 131
Mental illness, 2, 100, 105, 116, 127, 131
Movement therapy, 85, 113, 114, 123, 128
Music therapy, 123, 128
Myth, 2, 60

Normal indicators, 3–17, 90

Objects, recognizable, 3, 4, 13, 14, 21, 32, 38, 40, 57, 64, 89, 97, 102

Paints, 4, 12, 13, 22, 33, 34, 41, 44, 49, 61, 69, 88, 112
Parents, 1, 3, 19, 20, 23–25, 27, 31, 33, 40, 45, 59, 80, 87, 102, 106
Picasso, Pablo, 2
Pictorial stage, 14

Play, 19, 21, 26, 31, 37, 38, 47
Preadolescence, 87, 91–94, 121
Psychiatrist, 20, 124, 129
Psychoanalyst, 124
Psychologist, 10, 19, 20, 105, 118, 129

Rainbows, 50, 96
Reality, 15, 16, 65
Realistic proportions, See Size relationships
Regression, 50, 96
Role models, 63, 84, 97, 101, 107

School environment, 10, 15–17, 20, 23, 36, 55
Scribble, 6, 7, 11, 13, 22, 25, 27, 28, 32, 33, 34, 42, 50, 70, 102
Self-image, 52, 59–62, 67–70, 74, 80–82, 116, 118, 120
Sentence-picture stage/sequence, 13–15, 37–62
Sex differentiation, 2, 10, 17, 47, 48, 50, 52, 55, 60
    roles, 34, 47, 63, 68, 102, 106, 107
Sexual characteristics, 10, 107
Sexually abused children, 107, 108
Size relationships, 88, 97, 102, 111
Slanted images, 7, 104, 114
Society See Cultural influences
Stages (of development), 10, 25
Stick figures, 10, 95, 107
Storytelling (in drawings), 3, 7, 9, 12, 17, 40–42, 47, 53, 58, 102, 111
Stress, 17, 104, 105, 113, 114
Subject matter, 2, 40, 41, 75, 78, 87, 103
Sublimation, 19, 20
Symbolism, 41, 50, 56, 65, 67, 75, 103

"Tadpole figures," 13, 39
Teachers,
    art, 1, 3, 19–21, 23, 40, 45, 80, 87, 95, 106
Television, 9, 10, 50, 86, 107
"Terrible Twos," 27
Therapists, See also Art therapists, art therapy
Toilet training, 22, 27, 32, 37, 38, 62, 115
Trauma, 103–107
    physical, 104, 111, 112
Treatment, 9, 36, 47, 80, 81, 106, 114, 116, 120, 121, 125, 130

Van Gogh, Vincent, 2
Verbal development, 39, 49, 54, 63, 102

Warning signals, 7, 8, 35, 43–47, 53, 61, 71, 72, 78, 95–97
Word-shape stage/sequence, 12, 31, 32